ROCKIN THE JAVA INTERVIEW

The Ultimate JAVA Questions and Answers Reference

BECOME AN INTERVIEW MASTER, LEARN THE SECRET TO NEGOTIATING THE BEST SALARY AND A COMPREHENSIVE QUESTION AND ANSWER REFERENCE GUIDE FOR THE JAVA PROGRAMMING LANGUAGE. WHAT YOU DON'T KNOW IS COSTING YOU THOUSANDS OF DOLLARS EACH YEAR.

Greg Unger

Revision 2

Ordering Information

Quantity sales. Special discounts are available on quantity purchases by corporations, associations, and others. For details, contact us.

Orders by U.S. trade bookstores and wholesalers, please contact us.

Contact Information

Email address: businessathlete101@gmail.com

Website: http://www.thebestsellingbooks.org

Dedication

To you the reader. I write these books to pass on the knowledge I've gained over the years so you don't have to go through the trials and tribulations I had to.

Those who have a hard time remembering reference materials, this book is for you. I want you to succeed and I hope this book serves you well. Hopefully this levels the playing field and gets you the job you deserve. If you're going so far as to prepare yourself by reading this book, then I know you deserve it.

Table of Contents

Foreword

This book is broken up into sections by subject. You will find redundancy in some of the questions because they cross-pertain to multiple subjects. This makes it easier to skip to one subject or another without any cross dependency. Some of the questions are simple and some difficult. I would suggest you know the answers to all questions even if you just memorize the answer. The answers are short and to the point. If you feel you're lacking understanding of either the question or the answer, I urge you to do further reading. This is your profession and like any profession you need to become a master at what you do. You must know the language inside and out to be the best programmer you can be.

Don't worry if you need to re-read this book a few times. Most people will need to. I find it useful to have Visual Studio open when reading a book like this so I can review in practice things I learn while reading.

I tried to make this as comprehensive as possible without turning this into a reference guide. By no means is this book exhaustive. I could add another couple hundred pages and still not cover everything that could be covered, given the topics I've included. I'm not providing examples and samples to explain the answers. This question and answer reference is meant to get your mind to recall what you already know by giving you short, concise and easy to remember answers.

You'll find I don't group the questions in sections very often. I do this purposely to make your brain work harder in order to commit the information to memory.

CHAPTER 1   INTERVIEW BASICS

Your attitude

Let me start out by saying that your attitude is going to possibly play the biggest role in whether or not you get a great job. Because of this, prepare to be in the right state of mind before you sit down in front of an interviewer. As with almost all things, everyone gets better with practice. To be a top contender for a job, there's nothing better than completing a successful interview. And interviews can be intimidating prospects. Here are some suggestions to help you prepare to present yourself at your best.

Assess your skills and experiences

• Focus on three to four areas where your skills are the strongest. Knowing these will help you tell your interviewer why they should hire you.

• Practice describing your special talents and skills.

• Examine your work and education background. Look for skills and experiences that match the job description.

Create a list of relatable experiences

Employers want real examples of how you behave professionally.

• Identify examples that relate to the job description and where you have performed well using your skills and background.

Practice relating the experiences aloud

• Organize your thoughts and communicate clearly.

• Explain the situation.

• Describe your role or task.

• Describe the action you took

• Describe the results of your action.

• Include what you learned or what you might do differently in the future.

• Memorize your answers ahead of time but do NOT come off like the answers were memorized. No one wants to listen to a scripted, pre-recorded message but you also want to make sure you say the right thing.

Organizing your thoughts ahead of time and practicing them aloud will help you to feel more confident and communicate clearly in the interview. Be able to describe your useful skills in layman's terms in case your interviewer is not an expert in the field.

Example:

SITUATION: When I worked at the state library, many of the books were not filed correctly.

TASK: I was in charge of shelving books on three floors.

ACTION: I designed and proposed a new employee training method to my boss. I then presented the new method to the library assistants at the next staff meeting and everyone contributed ideas for the new training on shelving.

RESULT: After that meeting, there were fewer misplaced books, and customers asked fewer questions about finding missing books.

Participate in mock interviews

Practice the interview process to improve your communication and overcome nervousness and anxiety.

I'd go so far as to interview for jobs that I didn't even want, just to practice. You should be able to work on your demeanor and confidence level if you know, going into the interview, it isn't a job you want. Try new things and see what kind of response you get. When you don't have to worry about getting the job, you can focus on the fundamentals of being an interviewee.

Mock interviews will help you as well. You can do them with a friend or family member or in a mirror. You do whatever you have to do in order to get the job. This may sound like an odd thing to have to do but you won't think it odd when you get the job because you were prepared. Mock interviews help you get a feel for the interview process. They're also an opportunity to create a personality in your head that you can tap into whenever you're in this type of situation. Being a good interviewee is not about how smart you are, it's about how trained you are and how comfortable you are.

Believe me when I tell you that your comfort level will increase exponentially, the more training you have. Practice verbalizing how your background, skills and abilities fit the job you are interviewing for.

Behavior based interviews

Behavioral based interviews and questions have become standard practice. Recruiters ask for detailed descriptions on how you handled yourself in certain tasks and situations. The premise is that past behavior predicts future performance.

Themes for these types of questions include:

• Disagreements and conflicts with coworkers

• Innovative solutions to problems

• Qualities of a team leader and qualities of a team member

• Meeting or failing to meet deadlines

• Responding to criticism from a superior, co-worker, or classmate

• Persuading someone to accept your idea or concept

• Seeing a problem as an opportunity

• Adapting to a wide variety of people, situations, and/or environments

First impressions

First impressions are lasting ones. Often, they are made during the application process, even before the interview starts.

• Voice messages may be the employer's first impression of you.

   - The message on your answering machine or voice messaging should be courteous and professional.

   - Inform everyone who might answer your telephone that employment calls may come at any time. If you feel your roommates or members of household are unreliable, consider listing cell phone number. Be sure to manage your cell phone calls appropriately.

• Any time you interact with a potential employer or anyone on their staff, imagine that they are evaluating you.

• Be respectful in the way you dress and the way you act.

• Be positive, upbeat and professional when corresponding in person, by mail, phone or email.

• The person answering your questions or taking your application may be the CEO sitting in for the receptionist on a break. You never know!

Dress professionally for the position

• Research industry expectations regarding attire. This could be simply walking through the lobby of the workplace to observe how employees dress.

• Being dressed a little more formally than your Interviewer is acceptable. It shows respect for them, the position, and the company.

• Get plenty of sleep the night before. Your physical appearance will be at its best when you are alert and rested.

• Avoid perfumes and cologne. Your spouse or significant other may think you smell great, but the person who interviews you may not.

Plan ahead to be on time

• Map your route to the interview site.

• Know where to park and how to enter the building. (Do you need a photo id for security?)

• Plan to arrive 10-15 minutes early.

Introduce yourself politely to the receptionist

• Introduce yourself to the receptionist and tell them the purpose of your visit along with your name.

• Thank the receptionist for their assistance.

• The receptionist is one of the first employees of the company you will meet. While receptionists may not be making hiring decisions, they may mention their impressions to the interviewer.

Greet the interviewer cordially

• Greet your interviewer using Mr., Ms. or Mrs.

• Shake their hand.

• Tell the interviewer your name.

• Wait to be offered a seat before sitting.

• Relax yourself to appear friendly and be memorable.

Expect small talk

• Engage in the conversation, be responsive and take initiative.

• Don't worry if the conversation catches you off guard, the interviewer may be testing you to see how you react under pressure. Try to relax and respond naturally.

Many interviewers will begin the interview with casual conversation. This is a prelude to the interview where they examine your responses for qualities the company seeks. One of the greatest things you can do for yourself is to come up with 5 questions to talk about before-hand. On top of that, come up with witty answers and responses that you can make to further the discussion. If this is practiced enough, your first impression will be a great one.

The Interview

Your goal in an interview is to show and tell your best qualities to the interviewer. Understand that the interviewer 's goal is to evaluate you on criteria other than just your skill.

Points to Include in the Interview

- How you fit the job qualifications

- Why you want the job

- Why you want to work for the organization

- What you can contribute to the employer

- What you have learned about yourself and your work

More Tips

- Relate your background and accomplishments to the employer's needs.

- Don't talk about what was wrong with past jobs or past employers.

- Be sincere, positive, and honest with your answers.

- Have your resume and/or portfolio with you in a professional looking folder.

- Avoid mentioning financial concerns or personal problems.

- Take notes during the interview. Make sure you write down everyone you speak to, dates, times and questions asked. This will make you look diligent and engaged and will allow you to reflect upon the interview afterwards. Do not however, ignore the interviewer in order to take notes. Short-hand works wonders here.

How will you be evaluated?

Once the official part of an interview begins, interviewers will carefully listen and evaluate your responses. In addition to your knowledge about the job and interaction styles, they may look for the following qualities:

• How well do you understand the job and meet its qualifications?

• What skills do you use when interacting with others?

• How mentally alert and responsible are you?

• Can you draw proper inferences and conclusions during the course of the interview?

• Do you demonstrate a degree of intellectual depth when communicating, or is your thinking shallow and lacking depth?

• Have you used good judgment and common sense regarding your life planning up to this point?

• What is your capacity for problem solving?

• How well do you respond to stress and pressure?

Refrain from reciting memorized answers

• Present yourself as interested and naturally enthusiastic about the job, not rehearsed and flat.

• Research the position and organization to fit your skills to the job.

• Formulate concise answers.

Maintain proper body language.

• Sit up straight and look alert.

• Avoid fidgeting.

• Smile when appropriate.

• Maintain eye contact when being asked questions.

• Be aware of your tone of voice. Keep it energetic and avoid monotone answers.

Body language says more about an individual than their words. Match your body language to the impression you want to make.

Be prepared to ask questions

• Prepare 3-5 questions ahead of time. Again, being prepared here will behoove you. You will most likely ask the exact same questions in every interview, so be prepared ahead of time. The more inquisitive you are; the more interest you show.

• Ask about the duties of the job early so you can target your answers to the position.

• Pay attention to an employer's body language and watch how they react to your questions.

• Some employers may start the interview by asking whether you have any questions. Others will tell you that they have set aside time at the end for questions. Still, others might be comfortable with you asking questions throughout the interview.

If the interview is not going smoothly, don't panic.

• Some interviewers might test you to see how you handle stress.

• Stay positive.

• Ask your interviewer to repeat anything you don't understand so you can gather your thoughts.

Expect the unexpected

Sometimes questions are asked simply to see how you react.

• Pause briefly.

• Consider the question.

• Give a natural response.

During the interview, you may be asked some unusual questions. Surprise questions could range from, "Where do you see yourself in 5 years" to "If you could live in any time period, which one would it be and why?"

When unexpected questions come up, take note of them either immediately or as soon as possible. If one person asked this question, chances are another might so be prepared with a witty answer next time.

The closing is important

Concluding the interview

• Remain enthusiastic and courteous.

• Ask questions.

• Prepare questions ahead of time to help you decide if the position is suitable for you.

• Leave the interviewer(s) with three things that you would like them to remember about you.

This is also an opportunity to give additional information about your background that you think is pertinent to the position and that was not covered in the interview.

Questions to consider asking at the close of the interview

• What do you want the person in this position to accomplish within the first three months?

• Are there are any important skills needed for the job that have not been covered in the interview?

• What is the time frame for making the hiring decision?

- What are the core working hours?

- Does the position require me to be on call?

- How big is the team I would be working with?

- Is the environment laid back or a bit more rigid?

- What is the dress code?

Questions to avoid

- What is the starting salary?

- What are the vacation related perks, company benefits, or other perks of the job?

Wait for the interviewer to introduce these subjects. The best time to talk about salary is after you have been offered the job. You're then in a much better position to negotiate.

The conclusion of the interview

- This is usually indicated when the interviewer stands up.

- Shake hands and thank him/her for considering you.

• During the interview or shortly after, write down the name(s) of the interviewer(s) so you won't forget.

Follow up

• Thank your interviewer for their time before leaving.

• Send a thank you note via email or hand deliver within two days.

The goal of an interview is to leave a positive impression. Remind the interviewer of your interest, but avoid being annoying.

CHAPTER 2   HOW I GOT STARTED

When I was first starting out as a developer, I remember how excited I was at the mere thought of having any company interested in me. As time went on, and I moved from one company to the next, my salary grew almost exponentially and in a very short period of time. I would love to tell you that this happened because I'm a genius or that I had found the secret to the Jedi mind trick and was able to make people do what I wanted, but that would be "slightly" misleading.

The first developer job I ever had, my salary was $32,000 per year and I was extremely excited! If you do the math, you will find that dividing an annual salary by two gives you an approximate hourly rate of $16 per hour. $16 per hour to do what I love to do was amazing in my mind. Six months went by and even though I loved my job, I happened to see a job posting for another position at a startup company and decided to apply for it. It was a simple HTML developer position. They didn't even require me to be an expert. If I remember correctly, the job description said that I should have "some" knowledge of HTML. Keep in mind it was at a time when HTML was less trivial to know than it is today because standards were still being developed and the language itself was mildly esoteric.

Needless to say, I did the interview and amazingly enough, I got the job. I didn't find out until afterwards that the job paid $64,000 per year! That my friend is a two-fold increase in my salary in the first six months of being a developer! I was ecstatic! You have to believe me when I tell you that this is not an anomaly. You will see later in the book that I am a huge believer in the phrase "Fortis Fortuna Adiuvat".

The new company was amazing. Every benefit you could possibly imagine came with the job. From free gym memberships, to free food and soda all day long. There seemed to be no end. Who doesn't love and I mean LOVE free food and soda! We had lunch and dinner catered from nice restaurants and even kegs of beer brought in every Friday. This was the life and I was as happy as could be.

Fast-forward six months. My friend Bill sends me an email with a job description that a local company is hiring for. It's a six-month contract position with the possibility of extension. The pay is $50 per hour on w2 plus benefits. The job description stated that they wanted someone who had at least a few years of experience with Visual Basic and Desktop Applications development. I had neither. However, I had **some** knowledge of Visual Basic and was teaching myself the language from a book called "Learn Visual Basic in 21 Days" that I bought for $15 online.

I decided to interview just for the heck of it. Nothing ventured, nothing gained and fortune favors the bold kind of thing. In the interview, I know they're asking me fairly simple technical questions, none of which I answered correctly and all of which were over my head. I left the interview with my spirit broken and headed directly for 31 flavors to drown my sorrows in ice cream. I'm not really sure what the genetically encoded survival mechanism is that dictates "When I lose the game, it's time to get fat" but I assure you it is a strong one.

The next day, I'm back at my job, just as happy as could be and grateful for even having the job at all, as I sit stuffing myself with Snickers bars and soda. I check my email and see one from the company I just interviewed with that reads:

> *"Greg, thanks for coming in. We have decided that you are a good fit for this position and would like to know when you could start? The sooner the better. - David"*

My first reaction was that the email was a joke on me. No one could have interviewed any worse than I did, nor have any less technical acuity per the job description. It wasn't until much later in life that I understood that most jobs look for a good personality fit over technical expertise and that as long as you seemed confident and competent, you already won 90% of the battle.

Understand that I'm very money driven at this time, so now I start calculating what $50 per hour is, as compared to my current $64,000 per year salary. If we approximate, it turns out $50 per hour is roughly $100,000 per year! My jaw drops and frankly I must have blacked out, because I don't even remember sending the email back stating how pleased I was that they wanted me and that I could start in two weeks. I packed up everything at my desk, sent my letter of resignation and never looked back.

As a side note, that startup company, which had received millions of dollars of venture capital to the tune of about 30 million dollars, having no business plan or any way to make money, went "under" two weeks after I left. I remember talking to my boss a week before I left and telling him that I couldn't believe the company is seemingly doing so well when their only product generates no income whatsoever. I say seemingly because what company would be giving away so many benefits and perks to their employees unless they were doing really well? I wasn't any kind of business expert, but I figured it common sense that at some point one would need a product or service with which to make money. Well, it turns out, management wasn't so bright and less than bright people would give away benefits and perks when they weren't making any money whatsoever. I used to think that people in E-level positions had some hidden genius, but in reality, they're really no smarter than anyone else. This entire experience was definitely a lesson learned to say the least.

So let's look at the timeline here. My first year as a developer I start out making $32,000 per year and am as excited as can be. Six months goes by and I have already doubled my income to $64,000 per year. Six more months goes by and my salary has gone up 56.25% to $100,000 per year.

Think it ends there? Think again. Just four short months go by and I decide that it's time to start my own consulting business and to go find my own clients. I am a diligent researcher at heart. If I don't know something, I am very driven to learn. I will find as much literature as I can on how something is done. I will find any person I can to help me understand the ins and outs of any process. I do as much research as possible on how to start a company and even what kind of company i.e. LLC, S-Corp, C-Corp. After all was said and done, I started an LLC because it was fast, simple and cost virtually nothing to start or maintain.

Tip: Check your states corporation commission website for information on starting your own company, if you're so inclined. It is remarkably fast and painless to start an L.L.C. (Limited Liability Company) You may or may not want to do this if you do any contract work. There are tremendous tax advantages to starting your own business and writing off all of your business expenses.

I attained my first client through word of mouth. My per hour rate? $250 per hour working 40 hour weeks and being my own boss. A 500% increase in salary. I was raking it in, kicking ass and taking names.

Keep in mind, the economy at the time was ripe for this kind of rate and businesses seemed to have no end to their cash reserves. The hype to get their business online drove the need to hire good developers, who could get the job done and companies were willing to pay top dollar in order to get it done.

Luckily, I have always had one true asset about my personality that made all of this possible. The ability to read manuals, no matter how large they were, in one sitting. I absolutely despise reading books for leisure, I always have. There is just something about reading a book for fun that irks me and I could never truly pinpoint what that was, other than to say, I hate wasting my time for something just to get "fun" as my reward. I always need to be learning something new, or honing my skills, increasing my technical acuity and striving to be the better version of myself. Manuals were a way to learn something new, brush up on skills, have more knowledge, and for me, that was the best reward I could receive for my time. 500-page manual on Python? No problem, I'll be done by the end of the day and amazingly enough will retain enough of it to be functional. Sure I didn't memorize the whole thing, but I could learn enough to get the gist and actually start getting work done. By the end of the first week I was coding with the best of them. This is how it's always been for me. If I don't know something, I'll go out and learn it as quickly as possible. I'll try and master it and be the best I can be at it.

Between the age of 25 and 30 my net worth went from negative $22,000, racked up on my credit cards, to a $500,000+ net worth, with thoughts of retiring by the age of 32. I really thought that I just needed 2 million dollars to my name and no debt to retire. I found out later that 2 million dollars might not be enough to retire on. Also, when I say retire, I truly only define it as not having to "worry" about money. I don't think I could ever stop working. It just isn't me.

CHAPTER 3   THE ART OF SALARY NEGOTIATION

This section is incredibly important. It will make the difference between an income of $60,000 per year versus $100,000 per year just by changing your mindset. Your self-confidence, self-worth and perceived confidence will sell the best version of you for the most money every time. Employers hardly ever make their best offer first, and candidates who negotiate their salary almost always earns more than those who don't. I will use rate and salary interchangeably but know that when I talk about rate, I am talking about contract work versus salary which is compensation for full-time employment.

Tip: People who at least attempt to ask for a higher salary are perceived more positively, since they're demonstrating the skills the company wants to hire them for.

Let me stop here and make a quick point. I personally guarantee that if you follow the information in these first few chapters you will get more money for the same job hands down. On a brilliance scale from 1 to 10, I already know you're a 10 because you took the time to buy this book in order to make an additional $1k - $50k just by doing some research. I urge you to help me out, if, I have helped you out. Give me and my book rave reviews to your friends, colleagues and especially on websites like amazon.com and walmart.com. Now back to the fun.

Here's a step-by-step guide to negotiating your best salary yet:

Do your research

Before you go for an interview, you should find out what the market rates are for the job you're looking for. There are salary surveys available online, and if you're dealing with a recruitment agency, your recruiter should be able to advise you on the salary range for the position.

I'm going to repeat the following point a few times in this book to make my point. I strongly urge you to reply to every single recruiter who contacts you for the exact same position to find out what they will offer you as compensation for the position. You may be extremely surprised at the drastic range in compensation you are quoted!

Check online job boards and see what companies are offering for a particular city and area of expertise. I find that general reports on income by profession are grossly inaccurate and misleading. You need to see first-hand what companies are willing to pay. Chances are, the companies that do not post a salary or hourly rate are hiding the fact that they pay way too little. If there is no rate or salary, send them an email and apply whether you're interested or not and ask them what the rate or salary is just so you have a point of reference. The more information you have, the better you'll be able to sell yourself.

Think about what you want from the job, both in terms of the job itself and in terms of remuneration. This will help you appear more self-assured during the interview and salary negotiation process. The more specific your demands are, the better you're perceived and received by the employer.

The newest studies in business psychology show that you're perceived in an entirely different light when you come into an interview with an agenda and knowing exactly what you want out of the job. It demonstrates decisiveness, vision and forethought.

Talk money early

Tip: You should always ask about compensation before any interview. This is usually done in the pre-screen process before the real interview ever takes place. Don't waste your time and the company's time by not doing your due-diligence upfront.

While we all want to earn more when we change jobs, no employer wants to hire someone whose only motivation to change jobs is a higher salary. At the same time, your time is valuable and going into an interview for 4 hours only to find out it pays way less than you would even remotely find acceptable is a waste of your time and the company's time. Make sure you know exactly what the pay or pay range is up front. No matter what a recruiter or a company says, the company has a budget restriction that correlates to a range the hiring manager can work from. You need to know what this range is in order to get the best rate or salary you can.

So, how do you answer the inevitable interview question, "What salary are you looking for?" This is where your homework becomes invaluable. Hopefully, you'll know the market rates for the type of position you're looking for. It's better to give a range rather than a specific number — you don't want to give a salary that's perhaps lower than the employer is looking to pay, but you don't want to price yourself out of the market, either. Emphasize that you're primarily interested in finding the right job for you, and that salary isn't your main consideration. But, at the same time, my immediate response is always:

> *"What is the very best rate (or salary) for this position?"*

Believe me, you may have to ask a few times before you get an answer, but eventually you will get the information you want. The only reason why recruiters don't want to give you this information is because they want to make as much money as possible when placing you. If you don't mind giving away your money, then by all means, don't bother to ask questions. You and I both know, you want as much money as possible for your hard work and time.

Tip: Some recruiters will base what you should receive for the new position off of what you have recently made. This is unfair and frankly is wrong in my opinion. I either tell them that the information is not something I can talk about or I make up a number that matches what I expect from the new position. You are doing yourself a disservice by divulging information that will most likely be used against you.

Some recruiters have WAY more latitude than they let on.

The typical recruiter almost always has the ability to make the final decision on your compensation package. After you negotiate with them, they will need to go back and confirm the package with a hiring manager or supervisor.

In other words, the recruiter is going to sell you to the hiring manager. It's up to them to communicate why you deserve a higher salary. You want their support, because they're going to sell you at a rate that is commensurate with their impression of your personality and skill set. You can help the recruiter out by giving them justification for the compensation you're asking for and by not coming across as greedy or egotistical. The single biggest mistake that most candidates make when it comes to salary negotiation is telling the recruiter what they would be willing to accept. Most candidates don't like being pressured, so they simply blurt out a number they are willing to take — but you should never be the first one to give a number. One way to avoid this common mistake is to ask about the salary range the very first time you talk to a recruiter or hiring manager. If it's not enough, then be nice and give clear reasons for the compensation you do require. You're not battling against them; you're working with them. You would be amazed at what a little time spent negotiating can accomplish. You really have nothing to lose.

I have worked with some honest recruiters in the past and I have worked with some less than reputable ones and take my word, you need to run when you smell a rat. I remember taking a position for a company well under my normal rate just because I needed work fast and the job description made it sound easy with very little responsibility. I went back and forth with the recruiter trying to squeeze as much out of the rate as possible before finally accepting. I ended up with a rate that was $65 per hour and believe me it was a fight to the end to get this much. The recruiter also let me know that I would receive a sign on bonus if I stayed at least 30 days. This seemed sort of odd since I didn't even ask for it but I was more than willing to accept it under the circumstances.

By the third day on the job, my boss let it slip that the company was paying my recruiter $135 per hour! Let's do the math here. The recruiter is paying me $65 per hour and the company using the recruiter is paying the recruiter $135 per hour. The recruiter is making $70 per hour profit for every single hour I work. The recruiter is not only scamming me out of money but also scamming the company out of a much more experienced developer who would readily accept $100+ per hour versus $65 per hour. The company just got lucky that they hired me for that lesser rate. I guess that sign-on bonus wasn't so odd after all.

Needless to say, I re-negotiated the terms with the recruiter and was making over $100 per hour which was still far less than what the company was paying the recruiter! However, I was happier in the end, produced better work and stayed longer because of the additional money. This is a rare thing to have happen to anyone. I got lucky and although I don't recommend doing this, I will say that I would do it every single time, at the risk of losing the job. Sometimes you have to do things on principle, if you have the latitude to get away with it.

It's important to research the company and the position a recruiter is hiring for to try and get some semblance of what the position is actually paying. You will most likely receive emails from multiple recruiters for the exact same position and I urge you to respond to all of them with the following statement:

> "What's the very best rate (salary) for this position?"

I think you'll be extremely surprised at the responses you get. The exact same position for the exact same company will have a dramatically different range of compensation depending on who the recruiter is.

Example: I received 10 emails from different recruiters for a senior architect position with a company (Let's call the company XYZ) and to each recruiter, I responded asking what the very best rate for the position was. I was floored by the responses I received which were anywhere from $50 per hour to $125 per hour for the exact same position with the exact same job requisition number!

Shop around and find the best recruiter you can. It makes a dramatic difference. After all, a recruiter represents you and is tied to you for the duration of the contract. If it's a full time position, that's a different story but I leave it up to you to make the right choice as to whether you feel comfortable with the recruiter you're dealing with.

Believe that you CAN negotiate in this economy

Henry Ford said "Whether you think you can, or you think you can't--you're right." Your belief about your self-worth and your level of self-confidence can take you further than any other skill you have. You must believe you deserve the most money you can get from a position. Pretend you're your own talent manager and write down your strengths as if you were going to sell yourself. If you don't believe you deserve every penny you're worth, why should anyone else? You might as well stop reading now, because no amount of information is ever going to help you get ahead if you lack the self-confidence to walk the walk. If you believe it, you can achieve it.

Don't be afraid to ask — But don't demand, either

Know what your worth is and don't be afraid to ask for it. No one loses a job offer because they ask questions — however, you can have a job offer pulled because of the way you ask them. It's important that your salary or rate request is within the ballpark of the range for the position, so avoid giving a specific number until the employer is ready to make you an offer. Remember to be enthusiastic, polite and professional during negotiations. Communicate to your prospective employer through your tone of voice and demeanor, that your goal is a win-win solution. If you're too pushy, the employer may get the impression that you're not that interested in the job (or only interested in the money) and withdraw the offer.

Keep selling yourself

As you go through the interviewing and negotiating process, remind the employer how they'll benefit from your skills and experience. Let's say, for example, that the employer wants to offer $70K, but you're looking for minimum $90K base salary. Explain how they'd benefit by increasing your compensation.

For example:

> *"I realize you have a budget to worry about. However, I believe that with the desktop publishing and graphic design skills I bring to the position, you won't have to hire outside vendors to produce customer newsletters and other*

publications. That alone should produce far more than $20K in savings a year."

In other words, justify every additional dollar or benefit you request. Remember to do so by focusing on the employer's needs, not yours.

Make them jealous

If you're interviewing for other jobs, you might want to tell employers about those offers. This should speed up the acceptance process. If they know you have another offer, you'll seem more attractive to them, and it might help you negotiate a higher salary.

Tip: Sometimes when asked, I conjure other offers and interviews out of thin air. I do this to invoke a need of immediacy in order to get everyone moving as quickly as possible and to give myself some additional leverage when requesting compensation for a position. Get good at the bluff, it will serve you well.

Ask for a fair price

Again, you really need to ensure your compensation requests are reasonable and in line with the current marketplace. If the salary offer is below market value, you might want to gently suggest it's in the company's best interest to pay the going rate:

> *"The research that I've done indicates the going rate for a position such as this is $6K higher than this offer. I'd really love to work for you and I believe I can add a lot of value in this job; however, I can't justify doing so for less than market value. I think if you reevaluate the position and consider its importance to your bottom line, you'll find it's worth paying market price to get someone who can really make an impact quickly."*

Negotiate extras and be creative!

If the employer can't offer you the salary you want, think about other valuable options that might not cost them as much. You can look at negotiating holiday days (e.g. if new employees must work for 6 to 12 months before receiving paid holidays, ask that this restriction be waived.), ask for yearly salary reviews or negotiate a sign-on or performance bonus.

Be confident

Remember to use confident body language and speech patterns. When you make a salary request, don't go on and on, stating over and over why it's justified. Make your request and offer a short, simple explanation of why that amount is appropriate.

Tip: It's a smart negotiating strategy to ask for a few benefits or perks you don't want that badly. Then you can "give in" and agree to take the job without those added benefits, if, the employer meets all of your other requests.

Ideally, both parties in a negotiation should come away from the table feeling that they've won. This is especially true when you're dealing with salary negotiations. You want employers to have good feelings about the price paid for your services so that your working relationship begins on a positive note.

Keep track of what you have done well

The greatest tool that you have in any interview is proof. Keep examples of your best work, thank you notes from clients, awards or recognitions, and positive work evaluations.

Once you discover what is important to the company and how your skills can meet those needs, you can then use these items as proof of the value you can provide. It's a lot easier to get a higher salary when you have proof of why you deserve it.

Don't take it personally

Easier said than done? Not with practice. Maybe you'll get what you want. Maybe you won't. Life will move on either way. Most people will never have a negotiation that will make or break their life. Keep it real and don't get emotionally involved. If you ask for more than the job is willing to pay, let them call your bluff. It's going to be a numbers game and the more you play the game, the better you'll be at it and the more money you will make for the exact same 40 hours a week. Get the most money for your time!

CHAPTER 4   HOW TO BECOME A REMOTE WORKER

There are three ways to become a telecommuter or remote worker. The first, is if the job requirement states it's a telecommuting position. The second, is to convince your boss that should telecommute and the third, is to be your own boss, so you make the rules and deal only with clients who will allow telecommuting.

As a design project manager at a top Internet marketing firm, my dear friend Mary loved her job but couldn't stand the commute. When the price of gas soared to over $4 a gallon, she realized she was spending a small fortune getting to and from her office in downtown Los Angeles.

Mary had been with the company for four years and was already working at home one day a week. Now she chanced negotiating a permanent telecommuting arrangement with her boss.

"Because our company has a core value promoting a healthy work-life balance, all of our major software is available remotely. Because we have Internet phone lines, I thought my boss might be amenable to it," she says. "When I approached my boss, I mentioned my existing productivity working from home and how I felt that we could continue to measure that success while telecommuting full-time. I promised to be available to my clients during normal business hours and to return to the office two days a month for meetings or whenever there was an emergency."

Mary spent about 20 minutes coming up with and documenting this letter. That 20 minutes reaped enormous benefits that she would not have enjoyed otherwise, if it weren't for a little self-confidence and the belief that it was possible.

Mary has never been happier. "I get to work from home and also know I have a secure, reliable job." Her arrangement isn't unique. Organizations around the world are implementing telework with enthusiasm. According to a 2014 study by the American

Electronics Association, 47 million Americans already telecommute at least one day a week.

BT, a leading provider of communications solutions, hired its first home worker in 1986; today more than 70% of BT's employees benefit from flexible working. The company estimates that it has saved at least $500 million and has improved its productivity by between 15% and 31%.

How do you determine if telecommuting is for you? Michael Randall, a productivity expert, says the best candidates are people who are disciplined and self-motivated: "When your boss says, 'Here's a project, figure it out by this deadline,' do you get it done? Can you stay focused despite distractions and see a task through to completion?" He also says you need to be naturally organized and skilled at time management:

> *"People who work from home should be able to schedule realistically and prioritize correctly."*

If you think you fit the bill, your first step in making telecommuting a reality is to talk with someone in human resources to find out just how your organization's flexible work policy works. Don't despair if there's no official policy in place. There may be others in your department telecommuting successfully, and if you establish a high level of trust with your manager, broaching the issue won't be unreasonable.

To make the argument for telecommuting, prepare a written proposal that puts the organization first and addresses, upfront, the issues you know your boss will be concerned about. The key is to present teleworking as a benefit to the employer.

I was once offered a contracting position in which I explained that I could get the same amount of work done in three-quarters of the time from my own office–without the usual interruptions that comes with working in a room full of people. It would also be one fewer desk, phone and computer the company had to provide and one more notch in their belt as an earth-friendly employer that does what it can to keep cars off the road.

Your proposal should detail how you'll set up your home office, and it should assure your manager that you will have a clean, quiet and child-free work environment in which to complete your duties. Your boss will want to know that you have a fast Internet connection, a dedicated phone number and all the necessary supplies.

Suggest a trial period for the telecommuting arrangement after which you and your manager can evaluate how it's working. Once you're off and running, make a conscious effort to show your boss that you're cutting expenses and getting more work done faster. Make sure you're always accessible via e-mail and cellphone during the business day, and report often on where projects stand, so your boss can easily keep tabs on you.

Telecommuting shouldn't mean you never see the inside of the office building again. If you supervise other employees, or make presentations about your initiatives, or are a key participant in team meetings, show up in person as often as you can. Telecommuting must not compromise the critical workplace relationships you've spent time and energy building.

If you're currently job hunting and want to get into a telework situation right from the start, you can turn to a variety of websites that list such positions. FlexJobs.com, for example, is a low-cost subscription service that identifies and screens legitimate telecommuting jobs. Just be aware that telework positions tend to be much more competitive, so your resume should detail a history of independent work that produced stellar results.

When searching job boards online, you will want to use keywords like "Remote, virtual or telecommute" in order to find these kind of jobs. Important to note is that I find more often than not, the word "remote" is in many job descriptions that aren't telecommuting jobs at all, but deal with remote (outsourced) teams.

Also keep in mind that most remote positions pay less and are usually salary based, as opposed to hourly, but that doesn't mean you can't inquire about the position and ask if it can be done on a contractual basis. Be sure to send your references and a job history that includes all of the remote work you've done.

CHAPTER 5   TRAITS OF A BAD PROGRAMMER

I don't think anyone starts out thinking "I want to be a bad programmer." Unfortunately, I've uncovered some tautologies of human nature that go against the concept of excellence in almost everything we do as a species. The best example is that laziness is the default mode for most people. Laziness and the knowledge that most programmers can "get away" with doing things poorly, at most companies, is a strong pre-cursor to forming terrible habits that follow you the rest of your life. I've seen some truly disappointing code and watched the programmer's code software real-time in such a way as to make anyone cringe.

The following is a list of some of these bad habits:

1) You don't sharpen your axe before heading out into the forest to chop down the trees.

Let's setup an agreed upon context by which an understanding can be reached. I fully understand that sometimes there is no amount of before-hand thought that will afford you the same discovery as just trying to code something in prototype fashion, in order to do some due diligence, or solve a problem. But even a prototype should be an after-thought to at least doing some initial white-boarding when it comes to architecting software at any level. I am not talking about spending a lot of time figuring out how to write a method that will added two numbers. I'm talking about giving some forethought to how you design how the different pieces of your application will work.

2) You don't understand the fallibility of others. You don't understand that you are fallible.

We all make mistakes. Version control.

3) People should not have to know your entire history and perspective on life in order to understand your code.

Proper naming conventions and readable code.

4) You love to swim the pool of redundancy.

You write the same code over and over again instead of centralizing it and encapsulating it.

5) You don't think about anyone but yourself when you code.

I see it all the time. Programmers programming code in such a way as to just get things done as quickly as possible. Writing unmaintainable and unreadable code. So much so that the original programmer can't even read their own hieroglyphics. If you have ever worked on code and then walked away to do anything else only to have to come back to your very own code at some point later on in the future and had to take an enormous amount of time to figure out your own code than this is you. If you can't even understand what you did, why would you expect anyone else to know?

6) You don't understand the concept of teaching others to fish as opposed to giving them a fish when they are hungry.

7) Your ADHD (Attention Deficit) is in full force and controls every aspect of your life.

Scientists have done numerous studies on the human brain and what it is not only capable of but also what it excels at. These studies, over and over, point to the fact that "single-mindedness" allows the brain to do its very best work. Anyone who tells you that they are a hero because they can multi-task is like a drug junky who is telling you that drugs are the best and your life will be so much better with drugs in them.

CHAPTER 6 FUNDAMENTAL JAVA QUESTIONS AND ANSWERS

1. What is the difference between a constructor and a method?

A constructor is a member function of a class that is used to create objects of that class. It has the same name as the class itself, has no return type, and is invoked using the new operator.

A method is an ordinary member function of a class. It has its own name, a return type (which may be void), and is invoked using the dot operator.

2. What is the purpose of garbage collection in Java, and when is it used?

The purpose of garbage collection is to identify and discard objects that are no longer needed by a program so that their resources can be reclaimed and reused.

A Java object is subject to garbage collection when it becomes unreachable to the program in which it is used.

3. Describe synchronization in respect to multithreading.

With respect to multithreading, synchronization is the capability to control the access of multiple threads to shared resources.

Without synchronization, it's possible for one thread to modify a shared variable while another thread is in the process of using or updating that same shared variable. This usually leads to significant logic errors.

4. What is an abstract class?

An abstract class must be extended or sub-classed. It serves as a template and describes what something does. An abstract class cannot be instantiated (i.e. you may not call its constructor) and may contain static data.

Any class with an abstract method is automatically abstract itself, and must be declared as such. A class may be declared abstract even if it has no abstract methods. This prevents it from being instantiated.

5. What is the difference between an Interface and an Abstract class?

An abstract class can have instance methods that implement a default behavior. An Interface can only declare constants and instance methods, but cannot implement default behavior. All methods are implicitly abstract.

An interface has only public members which contain no implementation. An abstract class is a class which may have the usual flavors of class members (private, protected, etc.), but also may have abstract methods.

6. Explain different way of using thread?

The thread could be implemented by using runnable interface or by inheriting from the Thread class. The former is more advantageous, because when you are going for multiple inheritance, the only interface can help.

7. What is an Iterator?

Some of the collection classes provide traversal of their contents via a java.util.Iterator interface. This interface allows you to walk through a collection of objects, operating on each object in turn.

Remember when using Iterators that they contain a snapshot of the collection at the time the Iterator was obtained; generally, it is not advisable to modify the collection itself while traversing an Iterator.

8. **State the significance of public, private, protected, default modifiers both singly and in combination and state the effect of package relationships on declared items qualified by these modifiers.**

public: Public class is visible in other packages; field is visible everywhere (class must be public too)

private: Private variables or methods may be used only by an instance of the same class that declares the variable or method. A private feature may only be accessed by the class that owns the feature.

protected: Is available to all classes in the same package and also available to all subclasses of the class that owns the protected feature. This access is provided even to subclasses that reside in a different package from the class that owns the protected feature.

What you get by default ie, without any access modifier (i.e. public private or protected). It means that it is visible to all within a particular package.

9. What does static mean?

Static means one per class, not one for each object no matter how many instance of a class might exist. This means that you can use them without creating an instance of a class.Static methods are implicitly final, because overriding is done based on the type of the object, and static methods are attached to a class, not an object.

A static method in a superclass can be shadowed by another static method in a subclass, as long as the original method was not declared final. However, you can't override a static method with a non-static method. In other words, you can't change a static method into an instance method in a subclass.

10.   What is final class?

A final class can't be extended i.e. final class may not be sub-classed. A final method can't be overridden when its class is inherited. You can't change value of a final variable (is a constant).

11.   What if the main() method is declared as private?

The program compiles properly but at runtime it will give "main() method not public." message.

12.   What if the static modifier is removed from the signature of the main() method?

Program compiles. But at runtime throws an error "NoSuchMethodError".

13. What if I write static public void instead of public static void?

Program compiles and runs properly.

14. What if I do not provide the String array as the argument to the method?

Program compiles but throws a runtime error "NoSuchMethodError".

15. What is the first argument of the String array in main() method?

The String array is empty. It does not have any element. This is unlike C/C++ where the first element by default is the program name.

16. If I do not provide any arguments on the command line, then the String array of main() method will be empty or null?

It's empty, but not null.

17. How can one prove that the array is not null but empty using one line of code?

Print args.length. It will print 0. That means it is empty. But if it would have been null then it would have thrown a NullPointerException on attempting to print args.length.

18. What environment variables do I need to set on my machine in order to be able to run Java programs?

CLASSPATH and PATH are the two variables.

19. Can an application have multiple classes having main() method?

Yes, it's possible. While starting the application we mention the class name to be run. The JVM will look for the Main method only in the class whose name you have mentioned.

Hence there is not conflict amongst the multiple classes having main() method.

20. Can I have multiple main() methods in the same class?

No, the program will fail to compile. The compiler says that the main() method is already defined in the class.

21. Do I need to import java.lang package any time? Why?

No, it is loaded by default internally by the JVM.

22. Can I import same package/class twice? Will the JVM load the package twice at runtime?

One can import the same package or same class multiple times. Neither compiler nor JVM complains about it. And the JVM will internally load the class only once no matter how many times you import the same class.

23. What are Checked and UnChecked Exceptions?

A checked exception is some subclass of Exception (or Exception itself), excluding class RuntimeException and its subclasses. Making an exception checked forces client programmers to deal with the possibility that the exception will be thrown.

Example: IOException thrown by java.io.FileInputStream's read() method

Unchecked exceptions are RuntimeException and any of its subclasses. Class Error and its subclasses also are unchecked. With an unchecked exception, however, the compiler doesn't force client programmers either to catch the exception or declare it in a throws clause. In fact, client programmers may not even know that the exception could be thrown.

Example: StringIndexOutOfBoundsException thrown by String's charAt() method · Checked exceptions must be caught at compile time. Runtime exceptions do not need to be. Errors often cannot be.

24. What is overriding?

When a class defines a method using the same name, return type, and arguments as a method in its superclass, the method in the class overrides the method in the superclass.

When the method is invoked for an object of the class, it is the new definition of the method that is called, and not the method definition from superclass. Methods may be overridden to be more public, not more private.

25. Are the imports checked for validity at compile time? Example: will the code containing an import such as java.lang.ABCD compile?

Yes, the imports are checked for semantic validity at compile time. The code below will not compile. It will throw an error saying, cannot resolve symbol.

symbol: class ABCD

location: package io

import java.io.ABCD;

26. Does importing a package imports the sub-packages as well? Example: Does importing com.MyTest.* also import com.MyTest.UnitTests.*?

No you will have to import the sub-packages explicitly. Importing com.MyTest.* will import classes in the package MyTest only. It will not import any class in any of its sub-packages.

27. What is the difference between declaring a variable and defining a variable?

In declaration we just mention the type of the variable and its name. We do not initialize it. But defining means declaration + initialization.

Example: String s; is just a declaration while String s = new String ("abcd"); Or String s = "abcd"; are both definitions.

28. What is the default value of an object reference declared as an instance variable?

The default value will be null unless we define it explicitly.

29. Can a top level class be private or protected?

No. A top level class cannot be private or protected. It can have either "public" or no modifier. If it does not have a modifier it is supposed to have a default access.

If a top level class is declared as private the compiler will complain that the "modifier private is not allowed here". This means that a top level class cannot be private. Same is the case with protected.

30. What type of parameter passing does Java support?

In Java the arguments are always passed by value.

31. Primitive data types are passed by reference or pass by value?

Primitive data types are passed by value.

32. Objects are passed by value or by reference?

Java only supports pass by value. With objects, the object reference itself is passed by value and so both the original reference and parameter copy both refer to the same object.

33. *What is serialization?*

Serialization is a mechanism by which you can save the state of an object by converting it to a byte stream.

34. *How do I serialize an object to a file?*

The class whose instances are to be serialized should implement an interface Serializable. Then you pass the instance to the ObjectOutputStream which is connected to a fileoutputstream. This will save the object to a file.

35. *Which methods of Serializable interface should I implement?*

The serializable interface is an empty interface. It does not contain any methods. So we do not implement any methods.

36. *How can I customize the serialization process? i.e. how can one have a control over the serialization process?*

Yes, it's possible to have control over serialization process. The class should implement Externalizable interface. This interface contains two methods namely readExternal and writeExternal.

You should implement these methods and write the logic for customizing the serialization process.

37. What is the common usage of serialization?

Whenever an object is to be sent over the network, objects need to be serialized. Moreover, if the state of an object is to be saved, it needs to be serialized.

38. What is the Externalizable interface?

Externalizable is an interface which contains two methods readExternal and writeExternal. These methods give you a control over the serialization mechanism.

Thus if your class implements this interface, you can customize the serialization process by implementing these methods.

39. When you serialize an object, what happens to the object references included in the object?

The serialization mechanism generates an object graph for serialization. Thus it determines whether the included object references are serializable or not. This is a recursive process.

Thus when an object is serialized, all the included objects are also serialized along with the original object.

40. What one should take care of while serializing the object?

One should make sure that all the included objects are also serializable. If any of the objects is not serializable then it throws a NotSerializableException.

41. What happens to the static fields of a class during serialization?

There are three exceptions in which serialization does not necessarily read and write to the stream. These are

1. Serialization ignores static fields because they are not part of any particular state.

2. Base class fields are only handled if the base class itself is serializable.

3. Transient fields.

42. Does Java provide any construct to find out the size of an object?

No, there is not sizeof operator in Java. So there is not direct way to determine the size of an object directly in Java.

43. What are wrapper classes?

Java provides specialized classes corresponding to each of the primitive data types. These are called wrapper classes.

e.g. Integer, Character, Double etc.

44. Why do we need wrapper classes?

It's sometimes easier to deal with primitives as objects. Moreover, most of the collection classes store objects and not primitive data types. Wrapper classes also provide many utility methods.

Because of this, we need wrapper classes. And since we create instances of these classes, we can store them in any of the collection classes and pass them around as a collection. Also, we can pass them around as method parameters where a method expects an object.

45. What are checked exceptions?

Checked exception are those which the Java compiler forces you to catch.

Example: IOException are checked exceptions.

46. What are runtime exceptions?

Runtime exceptions are those exceptions that are thrown at runtime because of either wrong input data or because of wrong business logic etc. These are not checked by the compiler at compile time.

47. What is the difference between error and an exception?

An error is an irrecoverable condition occurring at runtime. Such as OutOfMemory error.

These JVM errors and you cannot repair them at runtime. While exceptions are conditions that occur because of bad input etc. Example: FileNotFoundException will be thrown if the specified file does not exist. Or a NullPointerException will take place if you try using a null reference.

In most of the cases it is possible to recover from an exception (probably by giving user a feedback for entering proper values etc.).

48. How to create custom exceptions?

Your class should extend class Exception, or some more specific type thereof.

49. If I want an object of my class to be thrown as an exception object, what should I do?

The class should extend from Exception class. Or you can extend your class from some more precise exception type also.

50. f my class already extends from some other class what should I do if I want an instance of my class to be thrown as an exception object?

One cannot do anything in this scenario, because Java does not allow multiple inheritance and does not provide any exception interface as well.

51. How does an exception permeate through the code?

An unhandled exception moves up the method stack in search of a matching When an exception is thrown from a code which is wrapped in a try block followed by one or more catch blocks, a search is made for matching catch block. If a matching type is found, then that block will be invoked. If a matching type is not found, then the exception moves up the method stack and reaches the caller method.

Same procedure is repeated if the caller method is included in a try catch block. This process continues until a catch block handling the appropriate type of exception is found. If it does not find such a block, then finally the program terminates.

52. What are the different ways to handle exceptions?

There are two ways to handle exceptions:

1. By wrapping the desired code in a try block followed by a catch block to catch the exceptions.

2. List the desired exceptions in the throws clause of the method and let the caller of the method handle those exceptions.

53. Is it necessary that each try block must be followed by a catch block?

It is not necessary that each try block must be followed by a catch block. It should be followed by either a catch block or a finally block. And whatever exceptions are likely to be thrown should be declared in the throws clause of the method.

54. If I write return at the end of the try block, will the finally block still execute?

Yes, even if you write return as the last statement in the try block and no exception occurs, the finally block will execute. The finally block will execute and then the control return.

55. If I write System.exit(0); at the end of the try block, will the finally block still execute?

No. In this case the finally block will not execute because when you say System.exit(0); the control immediately goes out of the program, and thus finally never executes.

56. How are Observer and Observable used?

Objects that subclass the Observable class maintain a list of observers. When an Observable object is updated it invokes the update() method of each of its observers to notify the observers that it has changed state.

The Observer interface is implemented by objects that observe Observable objects.

57. What is synchronization and why is it important?

With respect to multithreading, synchronization is the capability to control the access of multiple threads to shared resources.

Without synchronization, it is possible for one thread to modify a shared object while another thread is in the process of using or updating that object's value. This often leads to significant errors.

58. How does Java handle integer overflows and underflows?

It uses those low order bytes of the result that can fit into the size of the type allowed by the operation.

59. Does garbage collection guarantee that a program will not run out of memory?

Garbage collection does not guarantee that a program will not run out of memory. It is possible for programs to use up memory resources faster than they are garbage collected. It is also possible for programs to create objects that are not subject to garbage collection.

60. What is the difference between preemptive scheduling and time slicing?

Under preemptive scheduling, the highest priority task executes until it enters the waiting or dead states or a higher priority task comes into existence.

Under time slicing, a task executes for a predefined slice of time and then reenters the pool of ready tasks. The scheduler then determines which task should execute next, based on priority and other factors.

61. When a thread is created and started, what is its initial state?

A thread is in the ready state after it has been created and started.

62. What is the purpose of finalization?

The purpose of finalization is to give an unreachable object the opportunity to perform any cleanup processing before the object is garbage collected.

63.   What is the Locale class?

The Locale class is used to tailor program output to the conventions of a particular geographic, political, or cultural region.

64.   What is the difference between a while statement and a do statement?

A while statement checks at the beginning of a loop to see whether the next loop iteration should occur.

A do statement checks at the end of a loop to see whether the next iteration of a loop should occur. The do statement will always execute the body of a loop at least once.

65.   What is the difference between static and non-static variables?

A static variable is associated with the class as a whole rather than with specific instances of a class. Non-static variables take on unique values with each object instance.

66. How are this() and super() used with constructors?

this() is used to invoke a constructor of the same class. super() is used to invoke a superclass constructor.

67. What is daemon thread and which method is used to create the daemon thread?

Daemon thread is a low priority thread which runs intermittently in the back ground doing the garbage collection operation for the java runtime system.setDaemon method is used to create a daemon thread.

68. Can applets communicate with each other?

At this point in time applets may communicate with other applets running in the same virtual machine. If the applets are of the same class, they can communicate via shared static variables. If the applets are of different classes, then each will need a reference to the same class with static variables. In any case the basic idea is to pass the information back and forth through a static variable.

An applet can also get references to all other applets on the same page using the getApplets() method of java.applet.AppletContext. Once you get the reference to an applet, you can communicate with it by using its public members.

It is conceivable to have applets in different virtual machines that talk to a server somewhere on the Internet and store any data that needs to be serialized there. Then, when another applet needs this data, it could connect to this same server. Implementing this is non-trivial.

69. What are the steps in the JDBC connection?

While making a JDBC connection we go through the following steps:

Step 1: Register the database driver by using:

```
Class.forName(\" driver class for that
specific database\" );
```

Step 2: Now create a database connection using:

```
Connection con =
DriverManager.getConnection(url,username
,password);
```

Step 3: Now create a query using:

```
Statement stmt =
Connection.Statement(\"select * from
TABLE NAME\");
```

Step 4: Execute the query:

```
stmt.exceuteUpdate();
```

70. How does a try statement determine which catch clause should be used to handle an exception?

When an exception is thrown within the body of a try statement, the catch clauses of the try statement are examined in the order in which they appear. The first catch clause that is capable of handling the exception is executed. The remaining catch clauses are ignored.

71. Can an unreachable object become reachable again?

An unreachable object may become reachable again. This can happen when the object's finalize() method is invoked and the object performs an operation which causes it to become accessible to reachable objects.

72. What method must be implemented by all threads?

All tasks must implement the run() method, whether they are a subclass of Thread or implement the Runnable interface.

73. What are synchronized methods and synchronized statements?

Synchronized methods are methods that are used to control access to an object. A thread only executes a synchronized method after it has acquired the lock for the method's object or class.

Synchronized statements are similar to synchronized methods. A synchronized statement can only be executed after a thread has acquired the lock for the object or class referenced in the synchronized statement.

74. What modifiers are allowed for methods in an Interface?

Only public and abstract modifiers are allowed for methods in interfaces.

75. What are some alternatives to inheritance?

Delegation is an alternative to inheritance.

Delegation means that you include an instance of another class as an instance variable, and forward messages to the instance. It is often safer than inheritance because it forces you to think about each message you forward, because the instance is of a known class, rather than a new class, and because it doesn't force you to accept all the methods of the super class: you can provide only the methods that really make sense. On the other hand, it makes you write more code, and it is harder to re-use (because it is not a subclass).

76. What is the difference between preemptive scheduling and time slicing?

Under preemptive scheduling, the highest priority task executes until it enters the waiting or dead states or a higher priority task comes into existence. Under time slicing, a task executes for a predefined slice of time and then reenters the pool of ready tasks.

The scheduler then determines which task should execute next, based on priority and other factors.

77. What is the catch or declare rule for method declarations?

If a checked exception may be thrown within the body of a method, the method must either catch the exception or declare it in its throws-clause.

78. Is Empty .java file a valid source file?

Yes. An empty .java file is a perfectly valid source file.

79. Can a .java file contain more than one java classes?

Yes, a .java file may contain more than one java class, provided at most one of them is a public class.

80. Is String a primitive data type in Java?

No, String is not a primitive data type in Java, even though it is one of the most extensively used object. Strings in Java are instances of String class defined in java.lang package.

81. Is main a keyword in Java?

No, main is not a keyword in Java.

82. Is next a keyword in Java?

No, next is not a keyword.

83. Is delete a keyword in Java?

No, delete is not a keyword in Java. Java does not make use of explicit destructors the way C++ does.

84. Is exit a keyword in Java?

No. To exit a program explicitly you use the exit method in the System object.

85. What happens if you don't initialize an instance variable of any of the primitive types in Java?

Java by default initializes it to the default value for that primitive type. Thus an int will be initialized to 0(zero), a boolean will be initialized to false.

86. What will be the initial value of an object reference which is defined as an instance variable?

The object references are all initialized to null in Java. However, in order to do anything useful with these references, you must set them to a valid object, else you will get NullPointerExceptions everywhere you try to use such default initialized references.

87. What are the different scopes for Java variables?

The scope of a Java variable is determined by the context in which the variable is declared. Thus a java variable can have one of the three scopes at any given point in time.

1. Instance: - These are typical object level variables, they are initialized to default values at the time of creation of object, and remain accessible as long as the object accessible.

2. Local: - These are the variables that are defined within a method. They remain accessible only during the course of method execution. When the method finishes execution, these variables fall out of scope.

3. Static: - These are the class level variables. They are initialized when the class is loaded in JVM for the first time and remain there as long as the class remains loaded. They are not tied to any particular object instance.

88. What is the default value of the local variables?

The local variables are not initialized to any default value, neither primitives nor object references. If you try to use these variables without initializing them explicitly, the java compiler will not compile the code. It will complain ant the local variable not being initialized.

89. How many objects are created in the following piece of code?

MyClass c1, c2, c3;

c1 = new MyClass ();

c3 = new MyClass ();

Only 2 objects are created, c1 and c3. The reference c2 is only declared and not initialized.

90. Can a public class MyClass be defined in a source file named YourClass.java?

No. The source file name, if it contains a public class, must be the same as the public class name itself with a .java extension.

91. Can main() method be declared final?

Yes, the main() method can be declared final, in addition to being public static.

92. What is HashMap and Map?

Map is an Interface and Hashmap is the class that implements Map.

93. Difference between HashMap and HashTable?

The HashMap class is roughly equivalent to Hashtable, except that it's unsynchronized and permits nulls. (HashMap allows null values as key and value whereas Hashtable doesnt allow).

HashMap doesn't guarantee the order of the map will remain constant over time. HashMap is unsynchronized and Hashtable is synchronized.

94. Difference between Vector and ArrayList?

Vector is synchronized whereas arraylist is not.

95. Difference between Swing and Awt?

AWT are heavy-weight components. Swings are light-weight components. Hence swing works faster than AWT.

96. What will be the default values of all the elements of an array defined as an instance variable?

If the array is an array of primitive types, then all elements of the array will be initialized to the default value corresponding to that primitive type.

Example: All the elements of an array of int will be initialized to 0(zero), while that of boolean type will be initialized to false. Whereas if the array is an array of references (of any type), all the elements will be initialized to null.

CHAPTER 7   JAVA PRACTICE EXAM

Language Fundamentals Section

1. Which four options describe the correct default values for array elements of the types indicated?

```
int -> 0
String -> "null"
Dog -> null
char -> '\u0000'
float -> 0.0f
boolean -> true
```

A. 1, 2, 3, 4

B. 1, 3, 4, 5

C. 2, 4, 5, 6

D. 3, 4, 5, 6

2. Which one of these lists contains only Java programming language keywords?

A. class, if, void, long, Int, continue

B. goto, instanceof, native, finally, default, throws

C. try, virtual, throw, final, volatile, transient

D. strictfp, constant, super, implements, do

E. byte, break, assert, switch, include

3. Which will legally declare, construct, and initialize an array?

A. `int [] myList = {"1", "2", "3"};`

B. `int [] myList = (5, 8, 2);`

C. `int myList [] [] = {4,9,7,0};`

D. `int myList [] = {4, 3, 7};`

4. Which is a reserved word in the Java programming language?

A. method

B. native

C. subclasses

D. reference

E. array

5. Which is a valid keyword in java?

A. interface

B. string

C. Float

D. unsigned

6. Which three are legal array declarations?

```
int [] myScores [];
char [] myChars;
int [6] myScores;
Dog myDogs [];
Dog myDogs [7];
```

A. 1, 2, 4

B. 2, 4, 5

C. 2, 3, 4

D. All are correct.

7. *Which three piece of codes are equivalent to line 3?*

```
public interface Foo
{
    int k = 4; /* Line 3 */
}
final int k = 4;
public int k = 4;
static int k = 4;
abstract int k = 4;
volatile int k = 4;
protected int k = 4;
```

A. 1, 2 and 3

B. 2, 3 and 4

C. 3, 4 and 5

D. 4, 5 and 6

8. Which one of the following will declare an array and initialize it with five numbers?

A. `Array a = new Array(5);`

B. `int [] a = {23,22,21,20,19};`

C. `int a [] = new int[5];`

D. `int [5] array;`

9. Which three are valid declarations of a char?

```
char c1 = 064770;
char c2 = 'face';
char c3 = 0xbeef;
char c4 = \u0022;
char c5 = '\iface';
char c6 = '\uface';
```

A. 1, 2, 4

B. 1, 3, 6

C. 3, 5

D. 5 only

10. Which is the valid declarations within an interface definition?

A. `public double methoda();`

B. `public final double methoda();`

C. `static void methoda(double d1);`

D. `protected void methoda(double d1);`

11. Which one is a valid declaration of a boolean?

A. `boolean b1 = 0;`

B. `boolean b2 = 'false';`

C. `boolean b3 = false;`

D. `boolean b4 = Boolean.false();`

E. `boolean b5 = no;`

12. Which three are valid declarations of a float?

```
float f1 = -343;
float f2 = 3.14;
float f3 = 0x12345;
float f4 = 42e7;
float f5 = 2001.0D;
float f6 = 2.81F;
```

A. 1, 2, 4

B. 2, 3, 5

C. 1, 3, 6

D. 2, 4, 6

13. Which is a valid declarations of a String?

A. `String s1 = null;`

B. `String s2 = 'null';`

C. `String s3 = (String) 'abc';`

D. `String s4 = (String) '\ufeed';`

14. What is the numerical range of a char?

A. -128 to 127

B. -(215) to (215) - 1

C. 0 to 32767

D. 0 to 65535

Flow Control Section

15.   *Look at the following:*

```java
public void foo( boolean a, boolean b)
{
    if( a )
    {
        System.out.println("A"); /* Line
5 */
    }
    else if(a && b) /* Line 7 */
    {
        System.out.println( "A && B");
    }
    else /* Line 11 */
    {
        if ( !b )
        {
            System.out.println( "notB")
;
        }
        else
        {
```

```
            System.out.println( "ELSE" )
;

        }

    }

}
```

A. If a is true and b is true then the output is "A && B"

B. If a is true and b is false then the output is "notB"

C. If a is false and b is true then the output is "ELSE"

D. If a is false and b is false then the output is "ELSE"

16. Which two are acceptable types for x?

```
switch (x)
{
    default:
        System.out.println ("Hello");
}
```

1. byte
2. long
3. char
4. float
5. Short
6. Long

A. 1 and 3

B. 2 and 4

C. 3 and 5

D. 4 and 6

17. Which statement is true?

```java
public void test(int x)
{
    int odd = 1;
    if(odd) /* Line 4 */
    {
        System.out.println("odd");
    }
    else
```

```
    {
        System.out.println("even");
    }
}
```

A. Compilation fails.

B. "odd" will always be output.

C. "even" will always be output.

D. "odd" will be output for odd values of x, and "even" for even values.

18.   Which statement is true?

```
public class While
{
    public void loop()
    {
        int x= 0;
        while ( 1 ) /* Line 6 */
        {
            System.out.print("x plus one
is " + (x + 1)); /* Line 8 */
```

```
        }
    }
}
```

A. There is a syntax error on line 1.

B. There are syntax errors on lines 1 and 6.

C. There are syntax errors on lines 1, 6, and 8.

D. There is a syntax error on line 6.

Inner Class Section

19. Which is true about an anonymous inner class?

A. It can extend exactly one class and implement exactly one interface.

B. It can extend exactly one class and can implement multiple interfaces.

C. It can extend exactly one class or implement exactly one interface.

D. It can implement multiple interfaces regardless of whether it also extends a class.

20. Which one create an anonymous inner class from within class Bar?

```
class Boo
{
    Boo(String s) { }
    Boo() { }
}


class Bar extends Boo
```

```
{
    Bar() { }
    Bar(String s) {super(s);}
    void zoo()
    {
    // insert code here
    }
}
```

A. Boo f = new Boo(24) { };

B. Boo f = new Bar() { };

C. Bar f = new Boo(String s) { };

D. Boo f = new Boo.Bar(String s) { };

21.   Which is true about a method-local inner class?

A. It must be marked final.

B. It can be marked abstract.

C. It can be marked public.

D. It can be marked static.

22.   Which statement is true about a static nested class?

A. You must have a reference to an instance of the enclosing class in order to instantiate it.

B. It does not have access to non-static members of the enclosing class.

C. It's variables and methods must be static.

D. It must extend the enclosing class.

23.   Which constructs an anonymous inner class instance?

A. `Runnable r = new Runnable() { };`

B. `Runnable r = new Runnable(public void run() { });`

C. `Runnable r = new Runnable { public void run(){}};`

D. `System.out.println(new Runnable() {public void run() { }});`

24. Which statement, inserted at line 10, creates an instance of Bar?

```
class Foo
{
    class Bar{ }
}


class Test
{
    public static void main (String []
args)
    {
        Foo f = new Foo();
        /* Line 10: Missing statement ?
*/
    }
}
```

A. Foo.Bar b = new Foo.Bar();

B. Foo.Bar b = f.new Bar();

C. Bar b = new f.Bar();

D. Bar b = f.new Bar();

25. Which statement, if placed in a class other than MyOuter or MyInner, instantiates an instance of the nested class?

```
public class MyOuter
{
    public static class MyInner
    {
        public static void foo() { }
    }
}
```


A. `MyOuter.MyInner m = new MyOuter.MyInner();`

B. `MyOuter.MyInner mi = new MyInner();`

C.

`MyOuter m = new MyOuter();`

`MyOuter.MyInner mi = m.new MyOuter.MyInner();`

D. `MyInner mi = new MyOuter.MyInner();`

Assertions Section

26. What will be the output of the program?

```java
public class Test
{
    public static void main(String[] args)
    {
        int x = 0;
        assert (x > 0) ? "assertion failed" : "assertion passed" ;
        System.out.println("finished");
    }
}
```

A. finished

B. Compilation fails.

C. An AssertionError is thrown and finished is output.

D. An AssertionError is thrown with the message "assertion failed."

27. What causes compilation to fail?

```
public class Test
{
    public void foo()
    {
        assert false; /* Line 5 */
        assert false; /* Line 6 */
    }
    public void bar()
    {
        while(true)
        {
            assert false; /* Line 12 */
        }
        assert false;  /* Line 14 */
    }
}
```

A. Line 5

B. Line 6

C. Line 12

D. Line 14

28.   What will be the output of the program?

```java
public class Test
{
    public static int y;
    public static void foo(int x)
    {
        System.out.print("foo ");
        y = x;
    }
    public static int bar(int z)
    {
        System.out.print("bar ");
        return y = z;
    }
    public static void main(String []
args )
    {
        int t = 0;
        assert t > 0 : bar(7);
```

```
        assert t > 1 : foo(8); /* Line
18 */
        System.out.println("done ");
    }
}
```

A. bar

B. bar done

C. foo done

D. Compilation fails

29. What will be the output of the program (when you run with the -ea option)?

```
public class Test
{
    public static void main(String[]
args)
    {
        int x = 0;
        assert (x > 0) : "assertion
failed"; /* Line 6 */
        System.out.println("finished");
```

```
        }
}
```

A. finished

B. Compilation fails.

C. An AssertionError is thrown.

D. An AssertionError is thrown and finished is output.

30. Which line is an example of an inappropriate use of assertions?

```
public class Test2
{
    public static int x;
    public static int foo(int y)
    {
        return y * 2;
    }
    public static void main(String []
args)
    {
```

```
int z = 5;
assert z > 0; /* Line 11 */
assert z > 2: foo(z); /* Line 12
*/
if ( z < 7 )
    assert z > 4; /* Line 14 */
switch (z)
{
    case 4:
System.out.println("4 ");
    case 5:
System.out.println("5 ");
        default: assert z < 10;
}
if ( z < 10 )
        assert z > 4: z++; /* Line
22 */
    System.out.println(z);
  }
}
```

A. Line 11

B. Line 12

C. Line 14

D. Line 22

Declarations and Access Control Section

31. You want subclasses in any package to have access to members of a superclass. Which is the most restrictive access that accomplishes this objective?

A. public

B. private

C. protected

D. transient

32. Which of the following code fragments inserted, will compile?

```
public class Outer
{
    public void someOuterMethod()
    {
        //Line 5
    }
    public class Inner { }
        public static void main(String[]
argv)
```

```
    {
        Outer ot = new Outer();
        //Line 10
    }
}
```

A. new Inner(); //At line 5

B. new Inner(); //At line 10

C. new ot.Inner(); //At line 10

D. new Outer.Inner(); //At line 10

33. *Which two code fragments will compile?*

```
interface Base
{
    boolean m1 ();
    byte m2(short s);
}
```

1) interface Base2 implements Base {}

2) abstract class Class2 extends Base

```
{ public boolean m1(){ return true; }}
```

3) abstract class Class2 implements Base { }

4) abstract class Class2 implements Base

```
{ public boolean m1(){ return (7 > 4);
}}
```

5) abstract class Class2 implements Base

```
{ protected boolean m1(){ return (5 >
7) }}
```

A. 1 and 2

B. 2 and 3

C. 3 and 4

D. 1 and 5

34. Which three form part of correct array declarations?

1. `public int a [ ]`

2. `static int [ ] a`

3. `public [ ] int a`

4. `private int a [3]`

5. `private int [3] a [ ]`

6. `public final int [ ] a`

A. 1, 3, 4

B. 2, 4, 5

C. 1, 2, 6

D. 2, 5, 6

35.   What is the prototype of the default constructor?

`public class Test { }`

A. Test( )

B. Test(void)

C. public Test( )

D. public Test(void)

36. What is the most restrictive access modifier that will allow members of one class to have access to members of another class in the same package?

A. public

B. abstract

C. protected

D. synchronized

E. default access

37. Which of the following is/are legal method declarations?

1. protected abstract void m1();

2. static final void m1(){}

3. synchronized public final void m1() {}

4. private native void m1();

A. 1 and 3

B. 2 and 4

C. 1 only

D. All of them are legal declarations.

38.   Which cause a compiler error?

A. `int[ ] scores = {3, 5, 7};`

B. `int [ ][ ] scores = {2,7,6}, {9,3,45};`

C. `String cats[ ] = {"Fluffy", "Spot", "Zeus"};`

D. `boolean results[ ] = new boolean [] {true, false, true};`

E. `Integer results[ ] = {new Integer(3), new Integer(5), new Integer(8)};`

39.   Which three are valid method signatures in an interface?

1. `private int getArea();`

2. `public float getVol(float x);`

3. `public void main(String [] args);`

4. `public static void main(String []`
`args);`

5. `boolean setFlag(Boolean [] test);`

A. 1 and 2

B. 2, 3 and 5

C. 3, 4, and 5

D. 2 and 4

40. *You want a class to have access to members of another class in the same package. Which is the most restrictive access that accomplishes this objective?*

A. public

B. private

C. protected

D. default access

41. Which is valid in a class that extends class A?

```
class A
{
    protected int method1(int a, int b)
    {
        return 0;
    }
}
```

A. public int method1(int a, int b)
{return 0; }

B. private int method1(int a, int b) {
return 0; }

C. public short method1(int a, int b) {
return 0; }

D. static protected int method1(int a,
int b) { return 0; }

42. Which one creates an instance of an array?

A. int[ ] ia = new int[15];

B. `float fa = new float[20];`

C. `char[ ] ca = "Some String";`

D. `int ia[ ] [ ] = { 4, 5, 6 }, { 1,2,3 };`

43. Which two of the following are legal declarations for non-nested classes and interfaces?

1. `final abstract class Test {}`

2. `public static interface Test {}`

3. `final public class Test {}`

4. `protected abstract class Test {}`

5. `protected interface Test {}`

6. `abstract public class Test {}`

A. 1 and 4

B. 2 and 5

C. 3 and 6

D. 4 and 6

44. Which of the following class level (nonlocal) variable declarations will not compile?

A. `protected int a;`

B. `transient int b = 3;`

C. `private synchronized int e;`

D. `volatile int d;`

45. What is the widest valid returnType for methodA in line 3?

```
public class ReturnIt
{
    returnType methodA(byte x, double y)
/* Line 3 */
    {
        return (long)x / y * 2;
    }
}
```

A. int

B. byte

C. long

D. double

46. Which is valid in a class that extends class A?

```
class A
{
    protected int method1(int a, int b)
    {
        return 0;
    }
}
```

A. `public int method1(int a, int b)`
`{return 0; }`

B. `private int method1(int a, int b) {`
`return 0; }`

C. `public short method1(int a, int b) {`
`return 0; }`

D. `static protected int method1(int a, int b) { return 0; }`

Exceptions Section

47. What will be the output of the program?

```
public class Foo
{
    public static void main(String[]
args)
    {
        try
        {
            return;
        }
        finally
        {
            System.out.println(
"Finally" );
        }
    }
}
```

A. Finally

B. Compilation fails.

C. The code runs with no output.

D. An exception is thrown at runtime.

48. *What will be the output of the program?*

```
try
{
    int x = 0;
    int y = 5 / x;
}
catch (Exception e)
{
    System.out.println("Exception");
}
catch (ArithmeticException ae)
{
    System.out.println(" Arithmetic
Exception");
}
System.out.println("finished");
```

A. finished

B. Exception

C. Compilation fails.

D. Arithmetic Exception

49. What will be the output of the program?

```
public class X
{
    public static void main(String []
args)
    {
        try
        {
            badMethod();
            System.out.print("A");
        }
        catch (Exception ex)
        {
            System.out.print("B");
        }
        finally
        {
```

```
            System.out.print("C");
        }
        System.out.print("D");
    }
    public static void badMethod()
    {
        throw new Error(); /* Line 22 */
    }
}
```

A. ABCD

B. Compilation fails.

C. C is printed before exiting with an error message.

D. BC is printed before exiting with an error message.

50.   What will be the output of the program?

```
public class X
{
```

```java
    public static void main(String [] args)
    {
        try
        {
            badMethod();
            System.out.print("A");
        }
        catch (RuntimeException ex) /* Line 10 */
        {
            System.out.print("B");
        }
        catch (Exception ex1)
        {
            System.out.print("C");
        }
        finally
        {
            System.out.print("D");
        }
        System.out.print("E");
    }
```

```
    public static void badMethod()
    {
        throw new RuntimeException();
    }
}
```

A. BD

B. BCD

C. BDE

D. BCDE

51.   *What will be the output of the program?*

```
public class RTExcept
{
    public static void throwit ()
    {
        System.out.print("throwit ");
        throw new RuntimeException();
    }
    public static void main(String []
args)
```

```
    {
        try
        {
            System.out.print("hello ");
            throwit();
        }
        catch (Exception re )
        {
            System.out.print("caught ");
        }
        finally
        {
            System.out.print("finally
");
        }
        System.out.println("after ");
    }
}
```

A. hello throwit caught

B. Compilation fails

C. hello throwit RuntimeException caught after

D. hello throwit caught finally after

52. *What will be the output of the program?*

```
public class Test
{
    public static void aMethod() throws
Exception
    {
        try /* Line 5 */
        {
            throw new Exception(); /*
Line 7 */
        }
        finally /* Line 9 */
        {
            System.out.print("finally
"); /* Line 11 */
        }
    }
    public static void main(String
args[])
    {
```

```
        try
        {
            aMethod();
        }
        catch (Exception e)  /* Line 20
*/
        {
            System.out.print("exception
");
        }
        System.out.print("finished");  /*
Line 24 */
        }
}
```

A. finally

B. exception finished

C. finally exception finished

D. Compilation fails

53.   What will be the output of the program?

```java
public class X
{
    public static void main(String [] args)
    {
        try
        {
            badMethod();
            System.out.print("A");
        }
        catch (Exception ex)
        {
            System.out.print("B");
        }
        finally
        {
            System.out.print("C");
        }
        System.out.print("D");
    }
    public static void badMethod() {}
}
```

A. AC

B. BC

C. ACD

D. ABCD

54. *What will be the output of the program?*

```
public class X
{
    public static void main(String []
args)
    {
        try
        {
            badMethod(); /* Line 7 */
            System.out.print("A");
        }
        catch (Exception ex) /* Line 10
*/
        {
```

```
            System.out.print("B"); /*
Line 12 */
        }
        finally /* Line 14 */
        {
            System.out.print("C"); /*
Line 16 */
        }
        System.out.print("D"); /* Line
18 */
    }
    public static void badMethod()
    {
        throw new RuntimeException();
    }
}
```

A. AB

B. BC

C. ABC

D. BCD

55. *What will be the output of the program?*

```java
public class MyProgram
{
    public static void main(String
args[])
    {
        try
        {
            System.out.print("Hello
world ");
        }
        finally
        {
            System.out.println("Finally
executing ");
        }
    }
}
```

A. Nothing. The program will not compile because no exceptions are specified.

B. Nothing. The program will not compile because no catch clauses are specified.

C. Hello world.

D. Hello world Finally executing

56. *What will be the output of the program?*

```
class Exc0 extends Exception { }
class Exc1 extends Exc0 { } /* Line 2 */
public class Test
{
    public static void main(String args[])
    {
        try
        {
            throw new Exc1(); /* Line 9 */
        }
        catch (Exc0 e0) /* Line 11 */
        {
            System.out.println("Ex0 caught");
        }
        catch (Exception e)
```

```
        {

System.out.println("exception caught");
        }
    }
}
```

A. Ex0 caught

B. exception caught

C. Compilation fails because of an error at line 2.

D. Compilation fails because of an error at line 9.

Threading Section

57. What is the name of the method used to start a thread execution?

A. `init();`

B. `start();`

C. `run();`

D. `resume();`

58. Which two are valid constructors for Thread?

1. `Thread(Runnable r, String name)`

2. `Thread()`

3. `Thread(int priority)`

4. `Thread(Runnable r, ThreadGroup g)`

5. `Thread(Runnable r, int priority)`

A. 1 and 3

B. 2 and 4

C. 1 and 2

D. 2 and 5

59. Which three are methods of the Object class?

1. `notify();`

2. `notifyAll();`

3. `isInterrupted();`

4. `synchronized();`

5. `interrupt();`

6. `wait(long msecs);`

7. `sleep(long msecs);`

8. `yield();`

A. 1, 2, 4

B. 2, 4, 5

C. 1, 2, 6

D. 2, 3, 4

60. Which of the following line of code is suitable to start a thread?

```
class X implements Runnable
{
    public static void main(String
args[])
    {
        /* Missing code? */
    }
    public void run() {}
}
```

A. Thread t = new Thread(X);

B. Thread t = new Thread(X); t.start();

C. X run = new X(); Thread t = new Thread(run); t.start();

D. Thread t = new Thread(); x.run();

61. Which cannot directly cause a thread to stop executing?

A. Calling the `SetPriority()` method on a Thread object.

B. Calling the `wait()` method on an object.

C. Calling `notify()` method on an object.

D. Calling `read()` method on an InputStream object.

62. Which two of the following methods are defined in class Thread?

1. `start()`

2. `wait()`

3. `notify()`

4. `run()`

5. `terminate()`

A. 1 and 4

B. 2 and 3

C. 3 and 4

D. 2 and 4

63. Which three guarantee that a thread will leave the running state?

1. `yield()`

2. `wait()`

3. `notify()`

4. `notifyAll()`

5. `sleep(1000)`

6. `aLiveThread.join()`

7. `Thread.killThread()`

A. 1, 2 and 4

B. 2, 5 and 6

C. 3, 4 and 7

D. 4, 5 and 7

64. Which of the following will directly stop the execution of a Thread?

A. `wait()`

B. `notify()`

C. `notifyall()`

D. exits synchronized code

65. Which method must be defined by a class implementing the java.lang.Runnable interface?

A. `void run()`

B. `public void run()`

C. `public void start()`

D. `void run(int priority)`

66. Which will contain the body of the thread?

A. `run();`

B. `start();`

C. `stop();`

D. `main();`

67. Which method registers a thread in a thread scheduler?

A. `run();`

B. `construct();`

C. `start();`

D. `register();`

68. Assume the following method is properly synchronized and called from a thread A on an object B:

`wait(2000);`

After calling this method, when will the thread A become a candidate to get another turn at the CPU?

A. After thread A is notified, or after two seconds.

B. After the lock on B is released, or after two seconds.

C. Two seconds after thread A is notified.

D. Two seconds after lock B is released.

69.   Which of the following will not directly cause a thread to stop?

A. notify()

B. wait()

C. InputStream access

D. sleep()

70.   Which class or interface defines the wait(), notify(), and notifyAll() methods?

A. Object

B. Thread

C. Runnable

D. Class

71. Which of these will create and start this thread?

```java
public class MyRunnable implements Runnable
{
    public void run()
    {
        // some code here
    }
}
```

A. `new Runnable(MyRunnable).start();`

B. `new Thread(MyRunnable).run();`

C. `new Thread(new MyRunnable()).start();`

D. `new MyRunnable().start();`

Java.lang class

72. What is the value of "d" after this line of code has been executed?

```
double d = Math.round ( 2.5 +
Math.random() );
```

A. 2

B. 3

C. 4

D. 2.5

73. Which of the following would compile without error?

A. `int a = Math.abs(-5);`

B. `int b = Math.abs(5.0);`

C. `int c = Math.abs(5.5F);`

D. `int d = Math.abs(5L);`

74. Which of the following are valid calls to Math.max?

1. `Math.max(1,4)`

2. `Math.max(2.3, 5)`

3. `Math.max(1, 3, 5, 7)`

4. `Math.max(-1.5, -2.8f)`

A. 1, 2 and 4

B. 2, 3 and 4

C. 1, 2 and 3

D. 3 and 4

75. Look at the following:

```
public class Myfile
{
    public static void main (String[]
args)
    {
        String biz = args[1];
```

```
        String baz = args[2]
        String rip = args[3];
        System.out.println("Arg is " +
rip);
    }
}
```

Select how you would start the program to cause it to print: Arg is 2

A. java Myfile 222

B. java Myfile 1 2 2 3 4

C. java Myfile 1 3 2 2

D. java Myfile 0 1 2 3

Operators and Assignments Section

76. *What will be the output of the program?*

```
class PassA
{
    public static void main(String [] args)
    {
        PassA p = new PassA();
        p.start();
    }
    void start()
    {
        long [] a1 = {3,4,5};
        long [] a2 = fix(a1);
        System.out.print(a1[0] + a1[1] + a1[2] + " ");
        System.out.println(a2[0] + a2[1] + a2[2]);
    }
    long [] fix(long [] a3)
    {
        a3[1] = 7;
```

```
        return a3;
    }
}
```

A. 12 15

B. 15 15

C. 3 4 5 3 7 5

D. 3 7 5 3 7 5

77. *What will be the output of the program?*

```
class Test
{
    public static void main(String []
args)
    {
        Test p = new Test();
        p.start();
    }
    void start()
    {
        boolean b1 = false;
```

```
        boolean b2 = fix(b1);
        System.out.println(b1 + " " +
b2);
    }
    boolean fix(boolean b1)
    {
        b1 = true;
        return b1;
    }
}
```

A. true true

B. false true

C. true false

D. false false

78. What will be the output of the program?

```
class PassS
{
    public static void main(String []
args)
```

```
    {
        PassS p = new PassS();
        p.start();
    }
    void start()
    {
        String s1 = "slip";
        String s2 = fix(s1);
        System.out.println(s1 + " " +
s2);
    }
    String fix(String s1)
    {
        s1 = s1 + "stream";
        System.out.print(s1 + " ");
        return "stream";
    }
}
```

A. slip stream

B. slipstream stream

C. stream slip stream

D. slipstream slip stream

79.   What will be the output of the program?

```
class BitShift
{
    public static void main(String [] args)
    {
        int x = 0x80000000;
        System.out.print(x + " and  ");
        x = x >>> 31;
        System.out.println(x);
    }
}
```

A. -2147483648 and 1

B. 0x80000000 and 0x00000001

C. -2147483648 and -1

D. 1 and -2147483648

80. What will be the output of the program?

```
class Equals
{
    public static void main(String []
args)
    {
        int x = 100;
        double y = 100.1;
        boolean b = (x = y); /* Line 7
*/
        System.out.println(b);
    }
}
```

A. true

B. false

C. Compilation fails

D. An exception is thrown at runtime

81. What will be the output of the program?

```
class Test
```

```
{
    public static void main(String []
args)
    {
        int x=20;
        String sup = (x < 15) ? "small"
: (x < 22)? "tiny" : "huge";
        System.out.println(sup);
    }
}
```

A. small

B. tiny

C. huge

D. Compilation fails

82.   What will be the output of the program?

```
class Test
{
    public static void main(String []
args)
```

```
{
        int x= 0;
        int y= 0;
        for (int z = 0; z < 5; z++)
        {
            if (( ++x > 2 ) && (++y >
2))
            {
                x++;
            }
        }
        System.out.println(x + " " + y);
    }
}
```

A. 5 2

B. 5 3

C. 6 3

D. 6 4

83.   What will be the output of the program?

```
class Test
{
    public static void main(String [] args)
    {
        int x= 0;
        int y= 0;
        for (int z = 0; z < 5; z++)
        {
            if (( ++x > 2 ) || (++y > 2))
            {
                x++;
            }
        }
    System.out.println(x + " " + y);
    }
}
```

A. 5 3

B. 8 2

C. 8 3

D. 8 5

84. What will be the output of the program?

```
class Bitwise
{
    public static void main (String []
args)
    {
        int x = 11 & 9;
        int y = x ^ 3;
        System.out.println( y | 12 );
    }
}
```

A. 0

B. 7

C. 8

D. 14

85. What will be the output of the program?

```
class SSBool
```

```
{
    public static void main(String []
args)
    {
        boolean b1 = true;
        boolean b2 = false;
        boolean b3 = true;
        if ( b1 & b2 | b2 & b3 | b2 ) /*
Line 8 */
            System.out.print("ok ");
        if ( b1 & b2 | b2 & b3 | b2 | b1
) /*Line 10*/
            System.out.println("dokey");
    }
}
```

A. ok

B. dokey

C. ok dokey

D. No output is produced

E. Compilation error

86.   *What will be the output of the program?*

```
class SC2
{
    public static void main(String []
args)
    {
        SC2 s = new SC2();
        s.start();
    }
    void start()
    {
        int a = 3;
        int b = 4;
        System.out.print(" " + 7 + 2 + "
");
        System.out.print(a + b);
        System.out.print(" " + a + b + "
");
        System.out.print(foo() + a + b +
" ");
        System.out.println(a + b +
foo());
    }
```

```
    String foo()
    {
        return "foo";
    }
}
```

A. 9 7 7 foo 7 7foo

B. 72 34 34 foo34 34foo

C. 9 7 7 foo34 34foo

D. 72 7 34 foo34 7foo

87. What will be the output of the program?

```
class Test
{
    static int s;
    public static void main(String []
args)
    {
        Test p = new Test();
        p.start();
        System.out.println(s);
```

```
    }
    void start()
    {
        int x = 7;
        twice(x);
        System.out.print(x + " ");
    }
    void twice(int x)
    {
        x = x*2;
        s = x;
    }
}
```

A. 7 7

B. 7 14

C. 14 0

D. 14 14

88. *What will be the output of the program?*

```
class Two
```

```
{
    byte x;
}
class Pass0
{
    public static void main(String []
args)
    {
        Pass0 p = new Pass0();
        p.start();
    }
    void start()
    {
        Two t = new Two();
        System.out.print(t.x + " ");
        Two t2 = fix(t);
        System.out.println(t.x + " " +
t2.x);
    }
    Two fix(Two tt)
    {
        tt.x = 42;
        return tt;
```

```
        }
}
```

A. null null 42

B. 0 0 42

C. 0 42 42

D. 0 0 0

89.   *What will be the output of the program?*

```
class BoolArray
{
    boolean [] b = new boolean[3];
    int count = 0;
    void set(boolean [] x, int i)
    {
        x[i] = true;
        ++count;
    }
    public static void main(String []
args)
    {
```

```
        BoolArray ba = new BoolArray();
        ba.set(ba.b, 0);
        ba.set(ba.b, 2);
        ba.test();
    }
    void test()
    {
        if ( b[0] && b[1] | b[2] )
            count++;
        if ( b[1] && b[(++count - 2)] )
            count += 7;
        System.out.println("count = " +
count);
    }
}
```

A. count = 0

B. count = 2

C. count = 3

D. count = 4

90. What will be the output of the program?

```
public class Test
{
    public static void leftshift(int i,
int j)
    {
        i <<= j;
    }
    public static void main(String
args[])
    {
        int i = 4, j = 2;
        leftshift(i, j);
        System.out.printIn(i);
    }
}
```

A. 2

B. 4

C. 8

D. 16

Objects and Collections Section

91. *Suppose that you would like to create an instance of a new Map that has an iteration order that is the same as the iteration order of an existing instance of a Map. Which concrete implementation of the Map interface should be used for the new instance?*

A. TreeMap

B. HashMap

C. LinkedHashMap

D. The answer depends on the implementation of the existing instance.

92. *Which class does not override the equals() and hashCode() methods, inheriting them directly from class Object?*

A. `java.lang.String`

B. `java.lang.Double`

C. `java.lang.StringBuffer`

D. `java.lang.Character`

93. **Which collection class allows you to grow or shrink its size and provides indexed access to its elements, but whose methods are not synchronized?**

A. `java.util.HashSet`

B. `java.util.LinkedHashSet`

C. `java.util.List`

D. `java.util.ArrayList`

94. **You need to store elements in a collection that guarantees no duplicates are stored and all elements can be accessed in natural order. Which interface provides that capability?**

A. `java.util.Map`

B. `java.util.Set`

C. `java.util.List`

D. `java.util.Collection`

95. Which interface does java.util.Hashtable implement?

A. Java.util.Map

B. Java.util.List

C. Java.util.HashTable

D. Java.util.Collection

96. Which interface provides the capability to store objects using a key-value pair?

A. Java.util.Map

B. Java.util.Set

C. Java.util.List

D. Java.util.Collection

97. Which collection class allows you to associate its elements with key values, and allows you to retrieve objects in FIFO (first-in, first-out) sequence?

A. java.util.ArrayList

B. `java.util.LinkedHashMap`

C. `java.util.HashMap`

D. `java.util.TreeMap`

98.   Which collection class allows you to access its elements by associating a key with an element's value, and provides synchronization?

A. `java.util.SortedMap`

B. `java.util.TreeMap`

C. `java.util.TreeSet`

D. `java.util.Hashtable`

99.   Which is valid declaration of a float?

A. `float f = 1F;`

B. `float f = 1.0;`

C. `float f = "1";`

D. `float f = 1.0d;`

100. What line of code should replace the missing statement to make this program compile?

```
/* Missing Statement ? */
public class foo
{
    public static void
main(String[]args)throws Exception
    {
        java.io.PrintWriter out = new
java.io.PrintWriter();
        new
java.io.OutputStreamWriter(System.out,tr
ue);
        out.println("Hello");
    }
}
```

A. No statement required.

B. import java.io.*;

C. include java.io.*;

D. import java.io.PrintWriter;

101. What is the numerical range of char?

A. 0 to 32767

B. 0 to 65535

C. -256 to 255

D. -32768 to 32767

102. Which of the following are Java reserved words?

1. run

2. import

3. default

4. implement

A. 1 and 2

B. 2 and 3

C. 3 and 4

D. 2 and 4

Garbage Collection Section

103. When is the B object, created in line 3, eligible for garbage collection?

```
void start() {
    A a = new A();
    B b = new B();
    a.s(b);
    b = null; /* Line 5 */
    a = null;  /* Line 6 */
    System.out.println("start
completed"); /* Line 7 */
}
```

A. after line 5

B. after line 6

C. after line 7

D. There is no way to be absolutely certain.

104. Where will be the most chance of the garbage collector being invoked?

```
class HappyGarbage01
{
    public static void main(String
args[])
    {
        HappyGarbage01 h = new
HappyGarbage01();
        h.methodA(); /* Line 6 */
    }
    Object methodA()
    {
        Object obj1 = new Object();
        Object [] obj2 = new Object[1];
        obj2[0] = obj1;
        obj1 = null;
        return obj2[0];
    }
}
```

A. After line 9

B. After line 10

C. After line 11

D. Garbage collector never invoked in methodA().

105. At what point is the Bar object, created on line 6, eligible for garbage collection?

```
class Bar { }
class Test
{
    Bar doBar()
    {
        Bar b = new Bar(); /* Line 6 */
        return b; /* Line 7 */
    }
    public static void main (String args[])
    {
        Test t = new Test();   /* Line 11 */
        Bar newBar = t.doBar();   /* Line 12 */
        System.out.println("newBar");
        newBar = new Bar(); /* Line 14 */
```

```
        System.out.println("finishing");
/* Line 15 */
    }
}
```

A. after line 12

B. after line 14

C. after line 7, when doBar() completes

D. after line 15, when main() completes

106. When is the Demo object eligible for garbage collection?

```
class Test
{
    private Demo d;
    void start()
    {
        d = new Demo();
        this.takeDemo(d);  /* Line 7 */
    } /* Line 8 */
    void takeDemo(Demo demo)
```

```
        {

            demo = null;

            demo = new Demo();

        }

    }
```

A. After line 7

B. After line 8

C. After the start() method completes

D. When the instance running this code is made eligible for garbage collection.

107. After line 8 runs, how many objects are eligible for garbage collection?

```
public class X
{
    public static void main(String []
args)
    {
        X x = new X();
        X x2 = m1(x); /* Line 6 */
```

```
        X x4 = new X();
        x2 = x4; /* Line 8 */
        doComplexStuff();
    }
    static X m1(X mx)
    {
        mx = new X();
        return mx;
    }
}
```

A. 0

B. 1

C. 2

D. 3

CHAPTER 8 PRACTICE EXAM ANSWERS

Language Fundamentals Section

1. Answer: Option B

Explanation:

(1), (3), (4), (5) are the correct statements.

(2) is wrong because the default value for a String (and any other object reference) is null, with no quotes.

(6) is wrong because the default value for boolean elements is false.

2. Answer: Option B

Explanation:

All the words in option B are among the 49 Java keywords. Although goto reserved as a keyword in Java, goto is not used and has no function.

Option A is wrong because the keyword for the primitive int starts with a lowercase i.

Option C is wrong because "virtual" is a keyword in C++, but not Java.

Option D is wrong because "constant" is not a keyword. Constants in Java are marked static and final.

Option E is wrong because "include" is a keyword in C, but not in Java.

3. Answer: Option D

Explanation:

The only legal array declaration and assignment statement is Option D

Option A is wrong because it initializes an int array with String literals.

Option B is wrong because it uses something other than curly braces for the initialization.

Option C is wrong because it provides initial values for only one dimension, although the declared array is a two-dimensional array.

4. Answer: Option B

Explanation:

The word "native" is a valid keyword, used to modify a method declaration.

Option A, D and E are not keywords. Option C is wrong because the keyword for sub-classing in Java is extends, not 'subclasses'.

5. Answer: Option A

Explanation:

interface is a valid keyword.

Option B is wrong because although "String" is a class type in Java, "string" is not a keyword.

Option C is wrong because "Float" is a class type. The keyword for the Java primitive is float.

Option D is wrong because "unsigned" is a keyword in C/C++ but not in Java.

6. Answer: Option A

Explanation:

(1), (2), and (4) are legal array declarations. With an array declaration, you can place the brackets to the right or left of the identifier. Option A looks strange, but it's perfectly legal to split the brackets in a multidimensional array, and place them on both sides of the identifier. Although coding this way would only annoy your fellow programmers, for the exam, you need to know it's legal.

(3) and (5) are wrong because you can't declare an array with a size. The size is only needed when the array is actually instantiated (and the JVM needs to know how much space to allocate for the array, based on the type of array and the size).

7. Answer: Option A

Explanation:

(1), (2) and (3) are correct. Interfaces can have constants, which are always implicitly public, static, and final. Interface constant declarations of public, static, and final are optional in any combination.

8. *Answer: Option B*

Explanation:

Option B is the legal way to declare and initialize an array with five elements.

Option A is wrong because it shows an example of instantiating a class named Array, passing the integer value 5 to the object's constructor. If you don't see the brackets, you can be certain there is no actual array object! In other words, an Array object (instance of class Array) is not the same as an array object.

Option C is wrong because it shows a legal array declaration, but with no initialization.

Option D is wrong (and will not compile) because it declares an array with a size. Arrays must never be given a size when declared.

9. *Answer: Option B*

Explanation:

(1), (3), and (6) are correct. char c1 = 064770; is an octal representation of the integer value 27128, which is legal because it fits into an unsigned 16-bit integer. char c3 = 0xbeef; is a hexadecimal representation of the integer value 48879, which fits into an unsigned 16-bit integer. char c6 = '\uface'; is a Unicode representation of a character.

char c2 = 'face'; is wrong because you can't put more than one character in a char literal. The only other acceptable char literal that can go between single quotes is a Unicode value, and Unicode literals must always start with a '\u'.

char c4 = \u0022; is wrong because the single quotes are missing.

char c5 = '\iface'; is wrong because it appears to be a Unicode representation (notice the backslash), but starts with '\i' rather than '\u'.

10.   Answer: Option A

Explanation:

Option A is correct. A public access modifier is acceptable. The method prototypes in an interface are all abstract by virtue of their declaration, and should not be declared abstract.

Option B is wrong. The final modifier means that this method cannot be constructed in a subclass. A final method cannot be abstract.

Option C is wrong. static is concerned with the class and not an instance.

Option D is wrong. protected is not permitted when declaring a method of an interface. See information below.

Member declarations in an interface disallow the use of some declaration modifiers; you cannot use transient, volatile, or synchronized in a member declaration in an interface. Also, you may not use the private and protected specifiers when declaring members of an interface.

11.   *Answer: Option C*

Explanation:

A boolean can only be assigned the literal true or false.

12. Answer: Option C

Explanation:

(1) and (3) are integer literals (32 bits), and integers can be legally assigned to floats (also 32 bits). (6) is correct because (F) is appended to the literal, declaring it as a float rather than a double (the default for floating point literals).

(2), (4), and (5) are all doubles.

13. Answer: Option A

Explanation:

Option A sets the String reference to null.

Option B is wrong because null cannot be in single quotes.

Option C is wrong because there are multiple characters between the single quotes ('abc').

Option D is wrong because you can't cast a char (primitive) to a String (object).

14.   Answer: Option D

Explanation:

A char is really a 16-bit integer behind the scenes, so it supports 216 (from 0 to 65535) values.

Flow Control Section

15. **Answer: Option C**

Explanation:

Option C is correct. The output is "ELSE". Only when a is false do the output lines after 11 get some chance of executing.

Option A is wrong. The output is "A". When a is true, irrespective of the value of b, only the line 5 output will be executed. The condition at line 7 will never be evaluated (when a is true it will always be trapped by the line 12 condition) therefore the output will never be "A && B".

Option B is wrong. The output is "A". When a is true, irrespective of the value of b, only the line 5 output will be executed.

Option D is wrong. The output is "notB".

16. **Answer: Option A**

Explanation:

Switch statements are based on integer expressions and since both bytes and chars can implicitly be widened to an integer, these can also be used. Also shorts can be used. Short and Long are wrapper classes and reference types cannot be used as variables.

17. Answer: Option A

Explanation:

The compiler will complain because of incompatible types (line 4), the if expects a boolean but it gets an integer.

18. Answer: Option D

Explanation:

Using the integer 1 in the while statement, or any other looping or conditional construct for that matter, will result in a compiler error. This is old C Program syntax, not valid Java.

A, B and C are incorrect because line 1 is valid (Java is case sensitive so While is a valid class name). Line 8 is also valid because an equation may be placed in a String operation as shown.

Inner Classes Section

19. *Answer: Option C*

Explanation:

Option C is correct because the syntax of an anonymous inner class allows for only one named type after the new, and that type must be either a single interface (in which case the anonymous class implements that one interface) or a single class (in which case the anonymous class extends that one class).

Option A, B, D, and E are all incorrect because they don't follow the syntax rules described in the response for answer Option C.

20. *Answer: Option B*

Explanation:

Option B is correct because anonymous inner classes are no different from any other class when it comes to polymorphism. That means you are always allowed to declare a reference variable of the superclass type and have that reference variable refer to an instance of a subclass type, which in this case is an anonymous subclass of Bar. Since Bar is a subclass of Boo, it all works.

Option A is incorrect because it passes an int to the Boo constructor, and there is no matching constructor in the Boo class.

Option C is incorrect because it violates the rules of polymorphism—you cannot refer to a superclass type using a reference variable declared as the subclass type. The superclass is not guaranteed to have everything the subclass has.

Option D uses incorrect syntax.

21.   *Answer: Option B*

Explanation:

Option B is correct because a method-local inner class can be abstract, although it means a subclass of the inner class must be created if the abstract class is to be used (so an abstract method-local inner class is probably not useful).

Option A is incorrect because a method-local inner class does not have to be declared final (although it is legal to do so).

C and D are incorrect because a method-local inner class cannot be made public (remember-you cannot mark any local variables as public), or static.

22.   Answer: Option B

Explanation:

Option B is correct because a static nested class is not tied to an instance of the enclosing class, and thus can't access the nonstatic members of the class (just as a static method can't access nonstatic members of a class).

Option A is incorrect because static nested classes do not need (and can't use) a reference to an instance of the enclosing class.

Option C is incorrect because static nested classes can declare and define nonstatic members.

Option D is wrong because it just is. There's no rule that says an inner or nested class has to extend anything.

23.   *Answer: Option D*

Explanation:

D is correct. It defines an anonymous inner class instance, which also means it creates an instance of that new anonymous class at the same time. The anonymous class is an implementer of the Runnable interface, so it must override the run() method of Runnable.

A is incorrect because it doesn't override the run() method, so it violates the rules of interface implementation.

B and C use incorrect syntax.

24.   *Answer: Option B*

Explanation:

Option B is correct because the syntax is correct-using both names (the enclosing class and the inner class) in the reference declaration, then using a reference to the enclosing class to invoke new on the inner class.

Option A, C and D all use incorrect syntax. A is incorrect because it doesn't use a reference to the enclosing class, and also because it includes both names in the new.

C is incorrect because it doesn't use the enclosing class name in the reference variable declaration, and because the new syntax is wrong.

D is incorrect because it doesn't use the enclosing class name in the reference variable declaration.

25. **Answer: Option A**

Explanation:

MyInner is a static nested class, so it must be instantiated using the fully-scoped name of MyOuter.MyInner.

Option B is incorrect because it doesn't use the enclosing name in the new.

Option C is incorrect because it uses incorrect syntax. When you instantiate a nested class by invoking new on an instance of the enclosing class, you do not use the enclosing name. The difference between Option A and C is that Option C is calling new on an instance of the enclosing class rather than just new by itself.

Option D is incorrect because it doesn't use the enclosing class name in the variable declaration.

Assertions Section

26.   Answer: Option B

Explanation:

Compilation Fails. You can't use the Assert statement in a similar way to the ternary operator. Don't confuse.

27.   Answer: Option D

Explanation:

Option D is correct. Compilation fails because of an unreachable statement at line 14. It is a compile-time error if a statement cannot be executed because it is unreachable. The question is now, why is line 20 unreachable? If it's because of the assert, then surely line 6 would also be unreachable. The answer must be something other than assert.

Examine the following:

A while statement can complete normally if and only if at least one of the following is true:

- The while statement is reachable and the condition expression is not a constant expression with value true.

-There is a reachable break statement that exits the while statement.

The while statement at line 11 is infinite and there is no break statement therefore line 14 is unreachable. You can test this with the following code:

28.   Answer: Option D

Explanation:

The foo() method returns void. It is a perfectly acceptable method, but because it returns void it cannot be used in an assert statement, so line 18 will not compile.

29.   Answer: Option C

Explanation:

An assertion Error is thrown as normal giving the output "assertion failed". The word "finished" is not printed (ensure you run with the -ea option)

Assertion failures are generally labeled in the stack trace with the file and line number from which they were thrown, and also in this case with the error's detail message "assertion failed". The detail message is supplied by the assert statement in line 6.

30. **Answer: Option D**

Explanation:

Assert statements should not cause side effects. Line 22 changes the value of z if the assert statement is false.

Option A is fine; a second expression in an assert statement is not required.

Option B is fine because it is perfectly acceptable to call a method with the second expression of an assert statement.

Option C is fine because it is proper to call an assert statement conditionally.

Declarations and Access Control Section

31. *Answer: Option C*

Explanation:

Access modifiers dictate which classes, not which instances, may access features.

Methods and variables are collectively known as members. Method and variable members are given access control in exactly the same way.

private makes a member accessible only from within its own class

protected makes a member accessible only to classes in the same package or subclass of the class

default access is very similar to protected (make sure you spot the difference) default access makes a member accessible only to classes in the same package.

public means that all other classes regardless of the package that they belong to, can access the member (assuming the class itself is visible) final makes it impossible to extend a class, when applied to a method it prevents a method from being overridden in a subclass, when applied to a variable it makes it impossible to reinitialize a variable once it has been initialized

abstract declares a method that has not been implemented.

transient indicates that a variable is not part of the persistent state of an object.

volatile indicates that a thread must reconcile its working copy of the field with the master copy every time it accesses the variable.

After examining the above it should be obvious that the access modifier that provides the most restrictions for methods to be accessed from the subclasses of the class from another package is C - protected. A is also a contender but C is more restrictive, B would be the answer if the constraint was the "same package" instead of "any package" in other words the subclasses clause in the question eliminates default.

32.   Answer: Option A

Explanation:

Option A compiles without problem.

Option B gives error - non-static variable cannot be referenced from a static context.

Option C package ot does not exist.

Option D gives error - non-static variable cannot be referenced from a static context.

33.   Answer: Option C

Explanation:

(3) is correct because an abstract class doesn't have to implement any or all of its interface's methods. (4) is correct because the method is correctly implemented ((7 > 4) is a boolean).

(1) is incorrect because interfaces don't implement anything. (2) is incorrect because classes don't extend interfaces. (5) is incorrect because interface methods are implicitly public, so the methods being implemented must be public.

34.   Answer: Option C

Explanation:

(1), (2) and (6) are valid array declarations.

Option (3) is not a correct array declaration. The compiler complains with: illegal start of type. The brackets are in the wrong place. The following would work: public int[ ] a

Option (4) is not a correct array declaration. The compiler complains with: ']' expected. A closing bracket is expected in place of the 3. The following works: private int a []

Option (5) is not a correct array declaration. The compiler complains with 2 errors:

']' expected. A closing bracket is expected in place of the 3 and

<identifier> expected A variable name is expected after a[ ].

35.   Answer: Option C

Explanation:

Option A and B are wrong because they use the default access modifier and the access modifier for the class is public (remember, the default constructor has the same access modifier as the class).

Option D is wrong. The void makes the compiler think that this is a method specification - in fact if it were a method specification the compiler would spit it out.

36.   Answer: Option C

Explanation:

Option A and B are wrong because they use the default access modifier and the access modifier for the class is public (remember, the default constructor has the same access modifier as the class).

Option D is wrong. The void makes the compiler think that this is a method specification - in fact if it were a method specification the compiler would spit it out.

37.   Answer: Option D

Explanation:

All the given statements are legal declarations.

38.   Answer: Option B

Explanation:

Option B generates a compiler error: <identifier> expected. The compiler thinks you are trying to create two arrays because there are two array initializers to the right of the equals, whereas your intention was to create one 3 x 3 two-dimensional array.

To correct the problem and make option B compile you need to add an extra pair of curly brackets:

```
int [ ] [ ] scores = { {2,7,6}, {9,3,45} };
```

39.   Answer: Option B

Explanation:

(2), (3), and (5). These are all valid interface method signatures.

(1), is incorrect because an interface method must be public; if it is not explicitly declared public it will be made public implicitly. (4) is incorrect because interface methods cannot be static.

40.   Answer: Option D

Explanation:

The only two real contenders are C and D. Protected access Option C makes a member accessible only to classes in the same package or subclass of the class. While default access Option D makes a member accessible only to classes in the same package.

41.   Answer: Option A

Explanation:

Option A is correct - because the class that extends A is just simply overriding method1.

Option B is wrong - because it can't override as there are less access privileges in the subclass method1.

Option C is wrong - because to override, the return type needs to be an integer. The different return type means that the method is not overriding but the same argument list means that the method is not overloading. Conflict - compile time error.

Option D is wrong - because you can't override a method and make it a class method i.e. using static.

42. Answer: Option A

Explanation:

Option A is correct. It uses correct array declaration and correct array construction.

Option B is incorrect. It generates a compiler error: incompatible types because the array variable declaration is not correct. The array construction expects a reference type, but it is supplied with a primitive type in the declaration.

Option C is incorrect. It generates a compiler error: incompatible types because a string literal is not assignable to a character type variable.

Option D is wrong. It generates a compiler error <identifier> expected. The compiler thinks that you are trying to create two arrays because there are two array initializers to the right of the equals, whereas your intention was to create a 3 x 3 two-dimensional array.

43.   Answer: Option C

Explanation:

(3), (6). Both are legal class declarations.

(1) is wrong because a class cannot be abstract and final—there would be no way to use such a class. (2) is wrong because interfaces and classes cannot be marked as static. (4) and (5) are wrong because classes and interfaces cannot be marked as protected.

44.   Answer: Option C

Explanation:

Option C will not compile; the synchronized modifier applies only to methods.

Option A and B will compile because protected and transient are legal variable modifiers. Option D will compile because volatile is a proper variable modifier.

45. Answer: Option D

Explanation:

A, B and C are all wrong. Each of these would result in a narrowing conversion. Whereas we want a widening conversion, therefore the only correct answer is D. Don't be put off by the long cast, this applies only to the variable x and not the rest of the expression. It is the variable y (of type double) that forces the widening conversion to double.

Java's widening conversions are:

- From a byte to a short, an int, a long, a float, or a double.

- From a short, an int, a long, a float, or a double.

- From a char to an int, a long, a float, or a double.

- From an int to a long, a float, or a double.

- From a long to a float, or a double.

- From a float to a double.

46.   *Answer: Option A*

Explanation:

Option A is correct - because the class that extends A is just simply overriding method1.

Option B is wrong - because it can't override as there are less access privileges in the subclass method1.

Option C is wrong - because to override it, the return type needs to be an integer. The different return type means that the method is not overriding but the same argument list means that the method is not overloading. Conflict - compile time error.

Option D is wrong - because you can't override a method and make it a class method i.e. using static.

Exceptions Section

47.   *Answer: Option A*

Explanation:

If you put a finally block after a try and its associated catch blocks, then once execution enters the try block, the code in that finally block will definitely be executed except in the following circumstances:

1. An exception arising in the finally block itself.

2. The death of the thread.

3. The use of System.exit()

4. Turning off the power to the CPU.

I suppose the last three could be classified as VM shutdown.

48.   *Answer: Option C*

Explanation:

Compilation fails because ArithmeticException has already been caught. ArithmeticException is a subclass of java.lang.Exception, by time the ArithmeticException has been specified it has already been caught by the Exception class.

If ArithmeticException appears before Exception, then the file will compile. When catching exceptions the more specific exceptions must be listed before the more general (the subclasses must be caught before the superclasses).

49. Answer: Option C

Explanation:

An Error is thrown but not recognized (line 22), because the only catch attempts to catch an Exception and Exception is not a superclass of Error. Therefore, only the code in the finally statement can be run before exiting with a runtime error (Exception in thread "main" java.lang.Error).

50. Answer: Option C

Explanation:

A Run time exception is thrown and caught in the catch statement on line 10. All the code after the finally statement is run because the exception has been caught.

51. Answer: Option D

Explanation:

The main() method properly catches and handles the RuntimeException in the catch block, finally runs (as it always does), and then the code returns to normal.

A, B and C are incorrect based on the program logic described above. Remember that properly handled exceptions do not cause the program to stop executing.

52. Answer: Option C

Explanation:

This is what happens:

(1) The execution of the try block (line 5) completes abruptly because of the throw statement (line 7).

(2) The exception cannot be assigned to the parameter of any catch clause of the try statement therefore the finally block is executed (line 9) and "finally" is output (line 11).

(3) The finally block completes normally, and then the try statement completes abruptly because of the throw statement (line 7).

(4) The exception is propagated up the call stack and is caught by the catch in the main method (line 20). This prints "exception".

(5) Lastly program execution continues, because the exception has been caught, and "finished" is output (line 24).

53.   Answer: Option C

Explanation:

There is no exception thrown, so all the code with the exception of the catch statement block is run.

54.   Answer: Option D

Explanation:

(1) A RuntimeException is thrown, this is a subclass of exception.

(2) The exception causes the try to complete abruptly (line 7) therefore line 8 is never executed.

(3) The exception is caught (line 10) and "B" is output (line 12)

(4) The finally block (line 14) is always executed and "C" is output (line 16).

(5) The exception was caught, so the program continues with line 18 and outputs "D".

55.   Answer: Option D

Explanation:

Finally clauses are always executed. The program will first execute the try block, printing Hello world, and will then execute the finally block, printing Finally executing.

Option A, B, and C are incorrect based on the program logic described above. Remember that either a catch or a finally statement must follow a try. Since the finally is present, the catch is not required.

56. *Answer: Option A*

Explanation:

An exception Exc1 is thrown and is caught by the catch statement on line 11. The code is executed in this block. There is no finally block of code to execute.

Threading Section

57.   Answer: Option B

Explanation:

Option B is Correct. The start() method causes this thread to begin execution; the Java Virtual Machine calls the run method of this thread.

Option A is wrong. There is no init() method in the Thread class.

Option C is wrong. The run() method of a thread is like the main() method to an application. Starting the thread causes the object's run method to be called in that separately executing thread.

Option D is wrong. The resume() method is deprecated. It resumes a suspended thread.

58.   Answer: Option C

Explanation:

(1) and (2) are both valid constructors for Thread.

(3), (4), and (5) are not legal Thread constructors, although (4) is close. If you reverse the arguments in (4), you'd have a valid constructor.

59. Answer: Option C

Explanation:

(1), (2), and (6) are correct. They are all related to the list of threads waiting on the specified object.

(3), (5), (7), and (8) are incorrect answers. The methods isInterrupted() and interrupt() are instance methods of Thread.

The methods sleep() and yield() are static methods of Thread.

D is incorrect because synchronized is a keyword and the synchronized() construct is part of the Java language.

60. Answer: Option C

Explanation:

Option C is suitable to start a thread.

61. *Answer: Option C*

Explanation:

Option C is correct. notify() - wakes up a single thread that is waiting on this object's monitor.

62. *Answer: Option A*

Explanation:

(1) and (4). Only start() and run() are defined by the Thread class.

(2) and (3) are incorrect because they are methods of the Object class. (5) is incorrect because there's no such method in any thread-related class.

63. *Answer: Option B*

Explanation:

(2) is correct because wait() always causes the current thread to go into the object's wait pool.

(5) is correct because sleep() will always pause the currently running thread for at least the

duration specified in the sleep argument (unless an interrupted exception is thrown).

(6) is correct because, assuming that the thread you're calling join() on is alive, the thread calling join() will immediately block until the thread you're calling join() on is no longer alive.

(1) is wrong, but tempting. The yield() method is not guaranteed to cause a thread to leave the running state, although if there are runnable threads of the same priority as the currently running thread, then the current thread will probably leave the running state.

(3) and (4) are incorrect because they don't cause the thread invoking them to leave the running state.

(7) is wrong because there's no such method.

64. *Answer: Option A*

Explanation:

Option A is correct. wait() causes the current thread to wait until another thread invokes the notify() method or the notifyAll() method for this object.

Option B is wrong. notify() - wakes up a single thread that is waiting on this object's monitor.

Option C is wrong. notifyAll() - wakes up all threads that are waiting on this object's monitor.

Option D is wrong. Typically, releasing a lock means the thread holding the lock (in other words, the thread currently in the synchronized method) exits the synchronized method. At that point, the lock is free until some other thread enters a synchronized method on that object. Does entering/exiting synchronized code mean that the thread execution stops? Not necessarily because the thread can still run code that is not synchronized. I think the word directly in the question gives us a clue. Exiting synchronized code does not directly stop the execution of a thread.

65.   Answer: Option B

Explanation:

Option B is correct because in an interface all methods are abstract by default therefore they must be overridden by the implementing class. The Runnable interface only contains 1 method, the void run() method therefore it must be implemented.

Option A and D are incorrect because they are narrowing the access privileges i.e. package(default) access is narrower than public access.

Option C is not method in the Runnable interface therefore it is incorrect.

66.   *Answer: Option A*

Explanation:

Option A is Correct. The run() method to a thread is like the main() method to an application. Starting the thread causes the object's run method to be called in that separately executing thread.

Option B is wrong. The start() method causes this thread to begin execution; the Java Virtual Machine calls the run method of this thread.

Option C is wrong. The stop() method is deprecated. It forces the thread to stop executing.

Option D is wrong. Is the main entry point for an application.

67. Answer: Option C

Explanation:

Option C is correct. The start() method causes this thread to begin execution; the Java Virtual Machine calls the run method of this thread.

Option A is wrong. The run() method of a thread is like the main() method to an application. Starting the thread causes the object's run method to be called in that separately executing thread.

Option B is wrong. There is no construct() method in the Thread class.

Option D is wrong. There is no register() method in the Thread class.

68. Answer: Option A

Explanation:

Option A. Either of the two events (notification or wait time expiration) will make the thread become a candidate for running again.

Option B is incorrect because a waiting thread will not return to runnable when the lock is released, unless a notification occurs.

Option C is incorrect because the thread will become a candidate immediately after notification, not two seconds afterwards.

Option D is also incorrect because a thread will not come out of a waiting pool just because a lock has been released.

69.   *Answer: Option A*

Explanation:

Option A is correct. notify() - wakes up a single thread that is waiting on this object's monitor.

Option B is wrong. wait() causes the current thread to wait until another thread invokes the notify() method or the notifyAll() method for this object.

Option C is wrong. Methods of the InputStream class block until input data is available, the end of the stream is detected, or an exception is thrown. Blocking means that a thread may stop until certain conditions are met.

Option D is wrong. sleep() - Causes the currently executing thread to sleep (temporarily cease execution) for a specified number of milliseconds. The thread does not lose ownership of any monitors.

70. Answer: Option A

Explanation:

The Object class defines these thread-specific methods.

Option B, C, and D are incorrect because they do not define these methods. And yes, the Java API does define a class called Class, though you do not need to know it for the exam.

71. Answer: Option C

Explanation:

Because the class implements Runnable, an instance of it has to be passed to the Thread constructor, and then the instance of the Thread has to be started.

A is incorrect. There is no constructor like this for Runnable because Runnable is an interface, and it is illegal to pass a class or interface name to any constructor.

B is incorrect for the same reason; you can't pass a class or interface name to any constructor.

D is incorrect because MyRunnable doesn't have a start() method, and the only start() method that can start a thread of execution is the start() in the Thread class.

Java.lang Class Section

72.   Answer: Option B

Explanation:

The Math.random() method returns a number greater than or equal to 0 and less than 1. Since we can be sure that the sum of that number and 2.5 will be greater than or equal to 2.5 and less than 3.5, we can be sure that Math.round() will round that number to 3. So Option B is the answer.

73.   Answer: Option A

Explanation:

The return value of the Math.abs() method is always the same as the type of the parameter passed into that method.

In the case of A, an integer is passed in and so the result is also an integer which is fine for assignment to "int a".

The values used in B, C & D respectively are a double, a float and a long. The compiler will complain about a possible loss of precision if we try to assign the results to an "int".

74. **Answer: Option A**

Explanation:

(1), (2), and (4) are correct. The max() method is overloaded to take two arguments of type int, long, float, or double.

(3) is incorrect because the max() method only takes two arguments.

75. **Answer: Option C**

Explanation:

Arguments start at array element 0 so the fourth argument must be 2 to produce the correct output.

Operators and Assignments Section

76. *Answer: Option B*

Explanation:

Output: 15 15

The reference variables a1 and a3 refer to the same long array object. When the [1] element is updated in the fix() method, it is updating the array referred to by a1. The reference variable a2 refers to the same array object.

So Output: 3+7+5+" "3+7+5

Output: 15 15 Because Numeric values will be added

77. *Answer: Option B*

Explanation:

The boolean b1 in the fix() method is a different boolean than the b1 in the start() method. The b1 in the start() method is not updated by the fix() method.

78. Answer: Option D

Explanation:

When the fix() method is first entered, start()'s s1 and fix()'s s1 reference variables both refer to the same String object (with a value of

"slip"). Fix()'s s1 is reassigned to a new object that is created when the concatenation occurs (this second String object has a value of "slipstream"). When the program returns to start(), another String object is created, referred to by s2 and with a value of "stream".

79. Answer: Option A

Explanation:

Option A is correct. The >>> operator moves all bits to the right, zero filling the left bits. The bit transformation looks like this:

Before: 1000 0000 0000 0000 0000 0000 0000 0000

After: 0000 0000 0000 0000 0000 0000 0000 0001

Option C is incorrect because the >>> operator zero fills the left bits, which in this case changes the sign of x, as shown.

Option B is incorrect because the output method print() always displays integers in base 10.

Option D is incorrect because this is the reverse order of the two output numbers.

80.   Answer: Option C

Explanation:

The code will not compile because in line 7, the line will work only if we use (x==y) in the line. The == operator compares values to produce a boolean, whereas the = operator assigns a value to variables.

Option A, B, and D are incorrect because the code does not get as far as compiling. If we corrected this code, the output would be false.

81.   Answer: Option B

Explanation:

This is an example of a nested ternary operator. The second evaluation (x < 22) is true, so the "tiny" value is assigned to sup.

82. Answer: Option C

Explanation:

In the first two iterations x is incremented once and y is not because of the short circuit && operator. In the third and fourth iterations x and y are each incremented, and in the fifth iteration x is doubly incremented and y is incremented.

83. Answer: Option B

Explanation:

The first two iterations of the for loop both x and y are incremented. On the third iteration x is incremented, and for the first time becomes greater than 2. The short circuit or operator | | keeps y from ever being incremented again and x is incremented twice on each of the last three iterations.

84. *Answer: Option D*

Explanation:

The & operator produces a 1 bit when both bits are 1. The result of the & operation is 9. The ^ operator produces a 1 bit when exactly one bit is 1; the result of this operation is 10. The | operator produces a 1 bit when at least one bit is 1; the result of this operation is 14.

85. *Answer: Option B*

Explanation:

The & operator has a higher precedence than the | operator so that on line 8 b1 and b2 are evaluated together as are b2 & b3. The final b1 in line 10 is what causes that if test to be true. Hence it prints "dokey".

86. *Answer: Option D*

Explanation:

Because all of these expressions use the + operator, there is no precedence to worry about and all of the expressions will be evaluated from left to right. If either operand being evaluated is a String, the + operator will concatenate the two operands; if both operands are numeric, the + operator will add the two operands.

87. Answer: Option B

Explanation:

The int x in the twice() method is not the same int x as in the start() method. Start()'s x is not affected by the twice() method. The instance variable s is updated by twice()'s x, which is 14.

88. Answer: Option C

Explanation:

In the fix() method, the reference variable tt refers to the same object (class Two) as the t reference variable. Updating tt.x in the fix() method updates t.x (they are one in the same object). Remember also that the instance variable x in the Two class is initialized to 0.

89. Answer: Option C

Explanation:

The reference variables b and x both refer to the same boolean array. count is incremented for each call to the set() method, and once again when the first if test is true. Because of the && short circuit operator, count is not incremented during the second if test.

90.   *Answer: Option B*

Explanation:

Java only ever passes arguments to a method by value (i.e. a copy of the variable) and never by reference. Therefore, the value of the variable i remains unchanged in the main method.

If you're clever, you'll spot that 16 is 4 multiplied by 2 twice, (4 * 2 * 2) = 16. If you had 16 left shifted by three bits then 16 * 2 * 2 * 2 = 128. If you had 128 right shifted by 2 bits then 128 / 2 / 2 = 32. Keeping these points in mind, you don't have to go converting to binary to do the left and right bit shifts.

Objects and Collections Section

91.   *Answer: Option C*

Explanation:

The iteration order of a Collection is the order in which an iterator moves through the elements of the Collection. The iteration order of a LinkedHashMap is determined by the order in which elements are inserted.

When a new LinkedHashMap is created by passing a reference to an existing Collection to the constructor of a LinkedHashMap the Collection.addAll method will ultimately be invoked.

The addAll method uses an iterator to the existing Collection to iterate through the elements of the existing Collection and add each to the instance of the new LinkedHashMap.

Since the iteration order of the LinkedHashMap is determined by the order of insertion, the iteration order of the new LinkedHashMap must be the same as the interation order of the old Collection.

92.   *Answer: Option C*

Explanation:

java.lang.StringBuffer is the only class in the list that uses the default methods provided by class Object.

93.   *Answer: Option D*

Explanation:

All of the collection classes allow you to grow or shrink the size of your collection. ArrayList provides an index to its elements. The newer collection classes tend not to have synchronized methods. Vector is an older implementation of ArrayList functionality and has synchronized methods; it is slower than ArrayList.

94.   *Answer: Option B*

Explanation:

Option B is correct. A set is a collection that contains no duplicate elements. The iterator returns the elements in no particular order (unless this set is an instance of some class that provides a guarantee). A map cannot contain duplicate keys but it may contain duplicate values. List and Collection allow duplicate elements.

Option A is wrong. A map is an object that maps keys to values. A map cannot contain duplicate keys; each key can map to at most one value. The Map interface provides three collection views, which allow a map's contents to be viewed as a set of keys, collection of values, or set of key-value mappings. The order of a map is defined as the order in which the iterators on the map's collection views return their elements. Some map implementations, like the TreeMap class, make specific guarantees as to their order (ascending key order); others, like the HashMap class, do not (does not guarantee that the order will remain constant over time).

Option C is wrong. A list is an ordered collection (also known as a sequence). The user of this interface has precise control over where in the list each element is inserted. The user can access elements by their integer index (position in the list), and search for elements in the list. Unlike sets, lists typically allow duplicate elements.

Option D is wrong. A collection is also known as a sequence. The user of this interface has precise control over where in the list each element is inserted. The user can access elements by their integer index (position in the list), and search for elements in the list. Unlike sets, lists typically allow duplicate elements.

95.   Answer: Option A

Explanation:

Hash table based implementation of the Map interface.

96.   Answer: Option A

Explanation:

An object that maps keys to values. A map cannot contain duplicate keys; each key can map to at most one value.

97.   Answer: Option B

Explanation:

LinkedHashMap is the collection class used for caching purposes. FIFO is another way to indicate caching behavior. To retrieve LinkedHashMap elements in cached order, use the values() method and iterate over the resultant collection.

98.   Answer: Option D

Explanation:

Hashtable is the only class listed that provides synchronized methods. If you need synchronization great; otherwise, use HashMap, it's faster.

99.   Answer: Option A

Explanation:

Option A is valid declaration of float.

Option B is incorrect because any literal number with a decimal point u declare the computer will implicitly cast to double unless you include "F or f"

Option C is incorrect because it is a String.

Option D is incorrect because "d" tells the computer it is a double so therefore you are trying to put a double value into a float variable i.e there might be a loss of precision.

100. Answer: Option A

Explanation:

The usual method for using/importing the java packages/classes is by using an import statement at the top of your code. However, it is possible to explicitly import the specific class that you want to use as you use it which is shown in the code above. The disadvantage of this however is that every time you create a new object you will have to use the class path in the case "java.io" then the class name in the long run leading to a lot more typing.

101. Answer: Option B

Explanation:

The char type is integral but unsigned. The range of a variable of type char is from 0 to 216-1 or 0 to 65535. Java characters are Unicode, which is a 16-bit encoding capable of representing a wide range of international characters. If the most significant nine bits of a char are 0, then the encoding is the same as seven-bit ASCII.

102. Answer: Option B

Explanation:

(2) - This is a Java keyword

(3) - This is a Java keyword

(1) - Is incorrect because although it is a method of Thread/Runnable it is not a keyword

(4) - This is not a Java keyword the keyword is implements

Garbage Collection Section

103. Answer: Option D

104. Answer: Option D

Explanation:

Option D is correct. Garbage collection takes place after the method has returned its reference to the object. The method returns to line 6, there is no reference to store the return value. so garbage collection takes place after line 6.

Option A is wrong. Because the reference to obj1 is stored in obj2[0]. The Object obj1 still exists on the heap and can be accessed by an active thread through the reference stored in obj2[0].

Option B is wrong. Because it is only one of the references to the object obj1, the other reference is maintained in obj2[0].

Option C is wrong. The garbage collector will not be called here because a reference to the object is being maintained and returned in obj2[0].

105. Answer: Option B

Explanation:

Option B is correct. All references to the Bar object created on line 6 are destroyed when a new reference to a new Bar object is assigned to the variable newBar on line 14. Therefore the Bar object, created on line 6, is eligible for garbage collection after line 14.

Option A is wrong. This actually protects the object from garbage collection.

Option C is wrong. Because the reference in the doBar() method is returned on line 7 and is stored in newBar on line 12. This preserver the object created on line 6.

Option D is wrong. Not applicable because the object is eligible for garbage collection after line 14.

106. Answer: Option D

Explanation:

Option D is correct. By a process of elimination.

Option A is wrong. The variable d is a member of the Test class and is never directly set to null.

Option B is wrong. A copy of the variable d is set to null and not the actual variable d.

Option C is wrong. The variable d exists outside the start() method (it is a class member). So, when the start() method finishes the variable d still holds a reference.

107. Answer: Option B

Explanation:

By the time line 8 has run, the only object without a reference is the one generated as a result of line 6. Remember that "Java is pass by value," so the reference variable x is not affected by the m1() method.

Ref:
http://www.javaworld.com/javaworld/javaqa/2000-05/03-qa-0526-pass.html

108. Answer: Option C

Explanation:

Option A is wrong. This simply copies the object reference into the array.

Option B is wrong. The reference o is set to null, but, oa[0] still maintains the reference to the Float object.

Option C is correct. The thread of execution will then not have access to the object.

109. Answer: Option C

Explanation:

This is an example of the islands of isolated objects. By the time line 11 has run, the objects instantiated in lines 6 and 7 are referring to each other, but no live thread can reach either of them.

110. Answer: Option D

Explanation:

Option D is correct. When an object is no longer referenced, it may be reclaimed by the garbage collector. If an object declares a finalizer, the finalizer is executed before the object is reclaimed to give the object a last chance to clean up resources that would not otherwise be released. When a class is no longer needed, it may be unloaded.

Option A is wrong. I found 4 delete() methods in all of the Java class structure. They are:

1. delete() - Method in class java.io.File : Deletes the file or directory denoted by this abstract pathname.

2. delete(int, int) - Method in class java.lang.StringBuffer : Removes the characters in a substring of this StringBuffer.

3. delete(int, int) - Method in interface javax.accessibility.AccessibleEditableText : Deletes the text between two indices

4. delete(int, int) - Method in class : javax.swing.text.JTextComponent.AccessibleJTextComponent; Deletes the text between two indices

None of these destroy the object to which they belong.

Option B is wrong. I found 19 finalize() methods. The most interesting, from this questions point of view, was the finalize() method in class java.lang.Object which is called by the garbage collector on an object when garbage collection determines that there are no more references to the object. This method does not destroy the object to which it belongs.

Option C is wrong. But it is interesting. The Runtime class has many methods, two of which are:

1. getRuntime() - Returns the runtime object associated with the current Java application.

2. gc() - Runs the garbage collector. Calling this method suggests that the Java virtual machine expend effort toward recycling unused objects in order to make the memory they currently occupy available for quick reuse. When control returns from the method call, the virtual machine has made its best effort to recycle all discarded objects. Interesting as this is, it doesn't destroy the object.

Ending notes

At this point you should be an interview god or at least be better off than you when you started reading.

Remember, you shouldn't just memorize the answer without a thorough understanding of the concepts that lie behind the question and the answer. The best programmers are not always the smartest ones. The best programmers are the ones who spend the countless hours and days understanding not only the language they program in but the concepts that the language conveys. The language allows the programmer to implement abstractions and it is those abstractions that must be fully understood in order to implement the best applications.